Food and Agriculture Organization of the United Nations

UNECE

Reporting on Forests and Sustainable Forest Management in the Caucasus and Central Asia

Focus on Criteria and Indicators

GENEVA TIMBER AND FOREST STUDY PAPER 53

Developed under the project "Accountability Systems for Sustainable Forest Management in the Caucasus and Central Asia"

UNITED NATIONS

New York and Geneva, 2023

COPYRIGHT AND DISCLAIMER

The designations employed in UNECE and FAO publications, which are in conformity with United Nations practice, and the presentation of material therein do not imply the expression of any opinion whatsoever on the part of the United Nations Economic Commission for Europe (UNECE) or the Food and Agriculture Organization of the United Nations (FAO) concerning the legal status of any country, area or territory or of its authorities, or concerning the delimitation of its frontiers. The responsibility for opinions expressed in studies and other contributions rests solely with their authors, and publication does not constitute an endorsement by UNECE or FAO of the opinions expressed. Reference to names of firms and commercial products and processes, whether or not these have been patented, does not imply their endorsement by UNECE or FAO, and any failure to mention a particular firm, commercial product or process is not a sign of disapproval.

Copyright © 2023 United Nations and the Food and Agriculture Organization of the United Nations.

All rights reserved worldwide.

This work is co-published by the United Nations (UNECE) and the FAO.

ABSTRACT

Reporting on Forests and Sustainable Forest Management in the Caucasus and Central Asia – Focus on Criteria and Indicators provides an overview of status and developments in reporting on forests and sustainable forest management in five countries of the Caucasus and Central Asia (Armenia, Georgia, Kazakhstan, Kyrgyzstan and Uzbekistan). This reporting involves looking at forests in the context of the United Nations 2030 Agenda for Sustainable Development, recognizing the multiple roles forests play in achieving the United Nations Sustainable Development Goals.

Criteria and indicators are tools used to define, guide, monitor and assess progress towards sustainable forest management that help our understanding and inform discussions about sustainable forest management. They operate at the global, regional, international, national, subnational, and even at forest management unit levels; and are a basis for informed decision making, establishing national forest policy and facilitating international reporting.

A flexible framework of criteria and indicators helps to develop systems adjusted to the capacities, needs, and conditions in which they are applied. This publication provides information about the processes and results of national efforts in building criteria and indicator sets for countries of the region.

UNITED NATIONS PUBLICATION

Sales No. E.22.II.E.40

ISBN 978-92-1-117325-3

eISBN 978-92-1-002382-5

ISSN 1020-2269

eISSN 2518-6450

ECE/TIM/SP/53

Copyright © 2023 United Nations

All rights reserved worldwide.

United Nations publication issued by the Economic Commission for Europe (ECE).

Acknowledgements

This study was drafted as part of the project "Accountability Systems for Sustainable Forest Management in the Caucasus and Central Asia" implemented by the Joint UNECE/FAO Forestry and Timber Section and funded through the United Nations Development Account (UNDA). The following staff of the Joint UNECE/FAO Forestry and Timber Section managed the project and supported the finalization of the publication: Mr. Roman Michalak, Ms. Liliana Annovazzi-Jakab, Mr. Stephen Hatem and Mr. Bastian Stahl.

The ECE/FAO Forestry and Timber Section would like to recognize the authors, reviewers and the editor for their contributions to this publication.

Lead authors

Mr. Tamer Otrakcier
Ms. Stefanie Linser

Authors

Ms. Annemarie Bastrup-Birk
Ms. Marta Gaworska
Mr. Michael Köhl
Mr. Kari T. Korhonen
Mr. Andrzej Talarczyk

Reviewers

Ms. Eva Danielyan and Mr. Vardan Melikyan (Armenia)
Ms. Natia Tskhovrebadze and Mr. Merab Machavariani (Georgia)
Ms. Gaukhar Abuova (Kazakhstan)
Ms. Siuzanna Seideeva and Mr. Baktybek Yrsaliev (Kyrgyzstan)
Mr. Abduvokhid Zakhadullaev (Uzbekistan)

Editor

Mr. Douglas Clark (English version)

Contents

List of figures

List of tables

List of Acronyms and Abbreviations

ACTO	The Amazon Cooperation Treaty Organization
ASEAN	The Association of Southeast Asian Nations
C&I	Criteria and Indicators
CCA	The Caucasus and Central Asia
CSS	Communication Support Systems
DPSIR	driving force–pressure–state–impact–response
DSS	Decision Support Systems
ENFIN	European National Forest Inventory Network
FAO	Food and Agriculture Organization of the United Nations
FCN	Forest Communicators Network
FMU	Forest Management Unit
FOWL	Forest and Other Wooded Land
FPMSIS	Forest Policy and Management Support Information Systems
FRA	Global Forest Resources Assessment
FTS	UNECE/FAO Forestry and Timber Section
GIS	Geographic Information System
ICT	Information and communication technologies
ISS	Information-sharing Systems
ITTO	International Tropical Timber Organization
LFCC	The Low Forest Cover Countries
MAR	Monitoring, assessment, reporting
MCPFE	Ministerial Conference on the Protection of Forests in Europe (Forest Europe)
MP	Montreal Process
NFI	National Forest Inventory
NFP	National Forest Programme
NGO	Non-Governmental Organization
NWFP	Non-Wood Forest Products
REDD+	Reducing Emissions from Deforestation and Forest Degradation in Developing Countries, and the Role of Conservation, Sustainable Management of Forests and Enhancement of Forest Carbon Stocks
RMS	Resource Management Systems
SDGs	United Nations Sustainable Development Goals
SEMAFOR	System for the Evaluation of the Management of Forests
SFM	Sustainable Forest Management
UNCBD	United Nations Convention on Biological Diversity
UNCCD	United Nations Convention on Combating Desertification
UNECE	United Nations Economic Commission for Europe
UNFCCC	United Nations Framework Convention on Climate Change
UNFF	United Nations Forum on Forests

Overview

This publication provides an overview of reporting on forests and sustainable forest management in five countries of the Caucasus and Central Asia (Armenia, Georgia, Kazakhstan, Kyrgyzstan and Uzbekistan), which was a subject of the capacity-building project, "Accountability systems for sustainable forest management in the Caucasus and Central Asia", developed and implemented by the Joint UNECE/FAO Forestry and Timber Section and funded by the United Nations Development Account (UNDA).

The five countries joined this capacity-building project to develop their forest monitoring and reporting systems, primarily criteria and indicators (C&I) for sustainable forest management (SFM) on the national level. There were many common challenges in the forest sector in the project countries, among them, limited resources, a shortage of qualified personnel, a lack of coordination between sectors and little public or political awareness of the significance of the forest sector. The harsh climatic conditions expose forests to desertification, wildfires, pests and diseases. Over-grazing and illegal harvesting are the main causes of deforestation and forest degradation. National forestry organizations in the region have struggled with the lack of technical and financial capacity to maintain forest management planning systems and to conduct regular forest inventories. Although there have been visible improvements in recent years, problems of forest monitoring and systematic data collection prevail. Available data and forest-related statistics are often out of date and/or of insufficient quality.

The objective of the project was to strengthen the national capacity of project countries to develop national criteria, indicators and reporting, or accountability systems for sustainable forest management. By this, the project aimed to enable the countries to actively participate in international processes related to forests, fulfil related international reporting obligations on forests and forestry and contribute to the sustainable development of the forest sector towards a green economy.

The project focused on the achievement of two goals: (1) enhancing national knowledge of policymakers, national government experts, and other stakeholders, of the existing international best practice for the monitoring and reporting of sustainable forest management; and (2) enhancing national capacity to develop national monitoring, reporting and accountability systems.

Countries identified an overwhelming need to improve the capacity for forest inventories and monitoring. While data from old inventories, management plans and similar sources could be used, the countries recognized the need for, and benefit of improving forest management planning systems as well as of establishing regular inventories to meet national information requirements and international reporting obligations.

The countries acknowledged the value of C&I for SFM as an effective tool to show policymakers, decision makers, forestry employees, the scientific community, environmental organizations, entrepreneurs and other stakeholders how forests and forestry could contribute to achieving the SDGs. C&I for SFM also help to implement forest-related political commitments, for instance to conserve biodiversity and sustainably use of forests in harmony with cross-sectoral policies.

The project significantly improved the national knowledge on existing international best practice gained throughout the period of its implementation. Countries established links and cooperation with national stakeholders, using their feedback throughout the development process of the national C&I for SFM sets. All five project countries developed individual national criteria and indicator sets for sustainable forest management which reflect best the national circumstances and information needs (see annex).

National C&I for SFM sets developed through the project differ between countries in content and structure owing to varying conditions and circumstances on site. Given the dynamic nature of changing indicator needs, updates or amendments of some indicators can be expected at the implementation stage. The criteria, however, should remain unmodified to the extent possible.

Furthermore, the project significantly contributed to the renewal of regional cooperation in the forest sector and in forest management in general. The conferences and meetings, the developed guiding material and opportunities for informal consultations facilitated an alliance of professional contacts and exchanges among the experts and stakeholders of the Caucasus and Central Asia. In addition, the project supported the countries to contribute to the 2020 cycle of the FAO Forest Resources Assessment.

The collective efforts of key national experts, international experts, and the Joint UNECE/FAO Forestry and Timber Section project team strengthened existing capacities, allowing countries to report on sustainable forest management by using nationally aligned and internationally coherent C&I for SFM. The work contributed to a common understanding of SFM in line with international guidelines as a basis for future monitoring and reporting obligations. All five countries have finalized their national C&I for SFM sets and have elaborated comprehensive factsheets for each indicator as the basis for implementation.

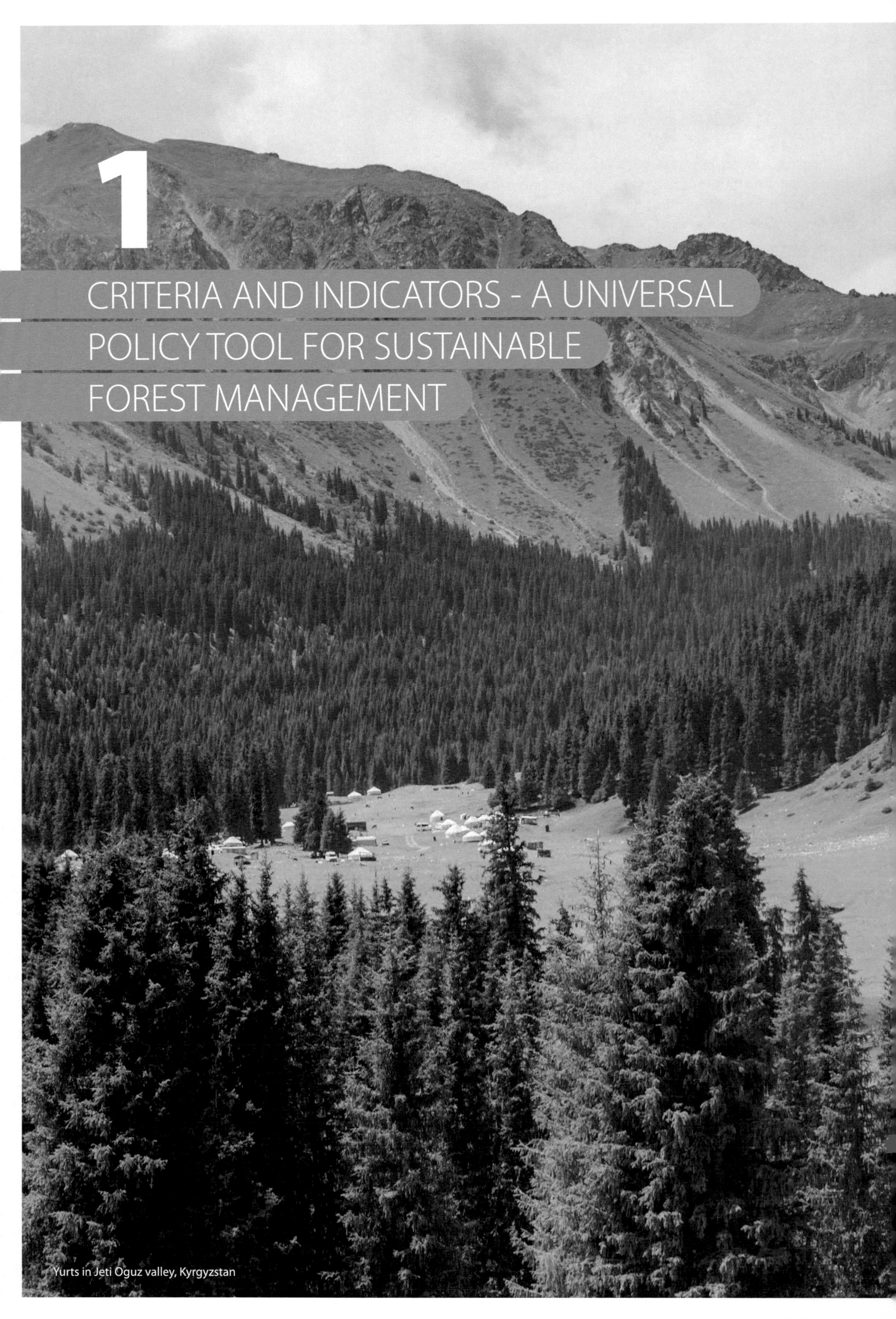

1

CRITERIA AND INDICATORS - A UNIVERSAL POLICY TOOL FOR SUSTAINABLE FOREST MANAGEMENT

Yurts in Jeti Oguz valley, Kyrgyzstan

1. Criteria and Indicators - a Universal Policy Tool for Sustainable Forest Management

Almost 30 years after their introduction, criteria and indicators for sustainable forest management (C&I for SFM) still rank high in public and political interest. C&I are still an increasingly common policy tool to implement sustainable forest management and to define related targets, which should improve key aspects of Sustainable Forest Management (SFM) monitoring, reporting and assessment.

What is SFM?

"A dynamic and evolving concept [that] aims to maintain and enhance the economic, social and environmental values of all types of forests, for the benefit of present and future generations" (UN, 2018).

Widely used definitions of Sustainable Forest Management (SFM) include:

"The stewardship and use of forests and forest lands in such a way, and at a rate, that maintains their biodiversity, productivity, regeneration capacity, vitality and their potential to fulfil now, and in the future, relevant ecological, economic and social functions, at local, national and global levels, and that does not cause damage to other ecosystems" (Ministerial Conference on the Protection of Forest in Europe (MCPFE, 1993).

The definitions highlight that while SFM will change over time, its purpose at a minimum is to maintain all forest benefits in perpetuity.

What are Criteria?

Broadly used definitions of criteria include:

"Criteria characterize or define the essential elements or set of conditions or processes by which sustainable forest management may be assessed" (MCPFE, 1998).

"Criteria define the essential elements against which sustainability is assessed, with due consideration paid to the productive, protective and social roles of forests and forest ecosystems. Each criterion relates to a key element of sustainability, and may be described by one or more indicators" (FAO, 2015a).

Thus, a criterion is a condition that should be met to confirm that forests are managed sustainably. This could be, for example, maintenance, enhancement, protection or conservation of the essential elements of SFM.

What are Indicators?

Indicators focus on aspects relevant within the respective criterion. Indicators may be quantitative or qualitative. Thus, respective figures are regularly monitored or descriptive information is surveyed focusing both on the status and changes of SFM. Commonly used definitions include:

"Indicators show changes over time for each criterion and demonstrate the progress made towards their specific objectives" (MCPFE, 1998).

"Indicators are parameters which can be measured and correspond to a particular criterion. They measure and help monitor the status and changes of forests in quantitative, qualitative and descriptive terms that reflect forest values as seen by those who defined each criterion" (FAO, 2015a).

"Sustainability indicators are science-based measures that provide a consistent approach to assess, monitor and report progress on SFM to a wide range of stakeholders and institutions, including governments, the private sector, non-governmental organizations, donor organizations, researchers and the public. Sustainability indicators can be useful to identify the changes in forest management practices required to maintain and improve healthy forests" (FAO, 2015b).

What is the difference between an indicator and other data?

Indicators reduce large quantities of data to a simpler form, retaining essential meaning for the questions that are being asked of the data or to be representative of the criteria they are aligned to. In short, an index or indicator is designed to simplify (Ott, 1978).

The result is a graded information system, reflecting the data pyramid in Figure 1 (Adrianse, 1995):

- Basic data: derived at the locus of sampling or other measurement.

- Processed information: statistically processed and harmonized data.

- Indicators: one- or two-dimensional figures, like forest area per capita.

- Indices: weighted, multidimensional aggregations with no unit, e.g. Human Development Index.

What are C&I for SFM?

Criteria and indicators are tools used to define, guide, monitor and assess progress towards SFM in a given context. C&I have emerged as a powerful tool in promoting SFM (FAO, 2015a). These are used in monitoring, evaluating and communicating progress towards more general targets formulated in the respective criteria (maintain, enhance…) or towards specific

FIGURE 1: Data Pyramid

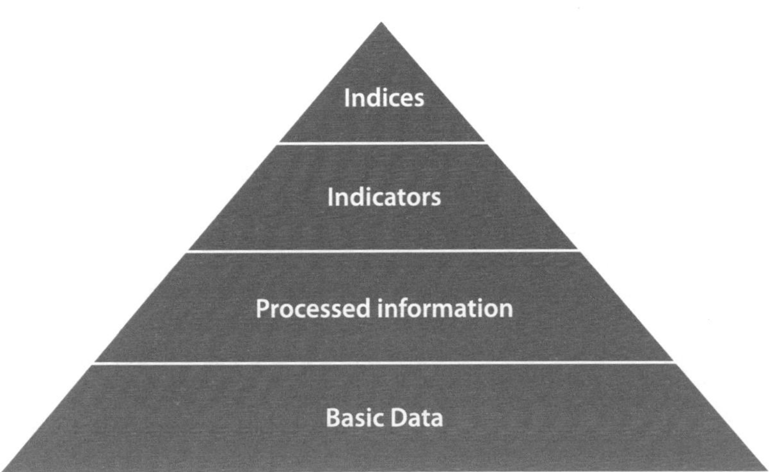

Source: Adrianse, 1995.

targets (quantitative or qualitative) set for each indicator. The comprehensive information that C&I provide help understanding and inform discussions about SFM. C&I for SFM operate at the global, regional, international, national, subnational, and even at forest management unit levels. C&I for SFM can be tailored to allow for differences within and between countries, regions or specific locations.

Why do we need C&I for SFM?

Indicators support decision-making. To implement the goals and targets of the United Nations 2030 Agenda for Sustainable Development, SDGs indicators[1] are used to monitor progress, inform policy and ensure accountability of all stakeholders.

The following United Nations Conventions adopted at the "United Nations Conference on Environment and Development in Rio de Janeiro" in 1992 indicators to show progress in the implementation of their targets. The Convention on Biological Diversity (CBD) has indicators to measure achievement against its 2020 Aichi Targets.[2] The UNFCCC has indicators to report achievement against climate targets.[3] The indicators of the UNCCD[4] provide information on progress towards achieving long-term objectives in areas affected by desertification, land degradation and drought. All these sets include some forest-related indicators.

In Europe, the Forest Europe process (Ministerial Conference on the Protection of Forests in Europe) developed a set of indicators that has since been revised three times to address emerging problems such as climate change or emerging issues such as ecosystem services or the bioeconomy. With 34 quantitative and 11 qualitative indicators, the pan-European indicators set[5] is the basis of the State of Europe's Forests reports and the national indicator sets of 23 European countries (Linser & Wolfslehner, 2021).

The Montreal Process Criteria and Indicators for the Conservation and Sustainable Management of Temperate and Boreal Forests[6] contain seven criteria and 54 indicators. The 12 member countries of the MP use this set of criteria and indicators to prepare country reports on progress toward sustainable forest management and, for some countries, as the basis for domestic processes to monitor, assess and report progress towards sustainable forest management (The Montreal Process, 2015).

The reporting system of the European Commission (EC) is based on sets of indicators (e.g. social indicators, health indicators, Natura-2000 indicators) and is supported in EU environmental policy by the Core-Set of Indicators of the European Environment Agency (EEA), as well as other specific indicator sets of the EEA[7].

---

1   SDGs Indicators: https://unstats.un.org/sdgs/

2   CBD Post-2020 framework: https://www.cbd.int/doc/c/0590/6ddd/ab6b9375338ff831dcf5541d/sbstta-23-inf-03-en.pdf

3   Global Set of Climate Change Statistics and Indicators: https://unstats.un.org/unsd/envstats/ClimateChange_StatAndInd_global.cshtml

4   UNCCD framework for Land Degradation Neutrality: https://www.unccd.int/sites/default/files/documents/2019-06/LDN_CF_report_web-english.pdf

5   Pan-European C&I set: https://foresteurope.org/sfm-criteria-indicators2/

6   Montréal Process C&I set: https://www.montrealprocess.org/documents/publications/techreports/MontrealProcessSeptember2015.pdf

7   European Environment Agency Indicators: https://www.eea.europa.eu/data-and-maps/indicators#c0=30&c12-operator=or&b_start=0

In 2015, an EC ad hoc working group of the Standing Forestry Committee discussed EU indicators within the EU Forest Strategy, and adopted the pan-European set of C&I for SFM of the Forest Europe process as sufficient for their purposes. The various EC Directorate Generals showed interest in key indicators for SFM and in subsets of forest-related indicators, e.g. for biodiversity, currently elaborated in the EuropaBON H2020 project[8].

Presently, thresholds or targets assigned to the various indicators are of interest and are requested for comprehensive sustainability assessments (Onida, 2021).

In addition, the bioeconomy and related concepts play a central role in the EC's current political agenda. This area focuses among others on (bio)technology, intensified use of natural resources, reducing dependency on non-renewable resources, and preventing and adapting to climate change, all which can be already mapped by forest-related indicators (Wolfslehner *et al.*, 2016). The EC Joint Research Centre recently developed a broad set of bioeconomy indicators, including forest-related indicators (Giuntoli *et al.*, 2020).

The 100 EUROSTAT Sustainable Development Indicators[9] are used to monitor and report progress towards the goals of the EU Sustainable Development Strategy and are structured along the 17 UN SDGs. They also contain forest-related indicators.

Indicators are strongly related to forest policy making. The highly developed forest indicators have the potential to inform other international, European or national indicator processes, such as sustainable bioeconomy or biodiversity indicators. This is true also for the development of national forest indicators, which still tend to focus only on European or international reporting obligations.

Short history of C&I for SFM

Agenda 21, the programme of action for the 21st century adopted at the United Nations Conference on Environment and Development in Rio de Janeiro in 1992, outlined an action plan for sustainable development at global, regional, national and local levels. The plan presented a challenge to measure sustainability worldwide. Chapter 40.4 of Agenda 21 proposed using indicators of sustainable development to provide a foundation for decision-making. The decades that followed saw the development of indicators covering a range of topics, from the global to the local level.

Since 1992, the evolution of national-level C&I for SFM has supported monitoring and reporting the state of forests and forestry. Their use has extended to also assessing the

sustainability of forest management. C&I guide forest sector development, identifying targets to release the full potential of SFM. They have broadened the scope of the forest sector to include social, economic and governance, as well as ecological aspects. Criteria for SFM at local, national, regional and international levels are tending to align, but sets of indicators for SFM range from the more generic at international and national levels to the more context-specific at the local level (Linser *et al.* 2018 a and b; UNECE/FAO, 2019).

Links to SDGs

In 2015, the United Nations General Assembly approved the 2030 Agenda for Sustainable Development, which contains 17 SDGs and 169 targets to be achieved by all countries by 2020 or 2030. There are 231 unique indicators[10] to assess progress against set targets.

Forests play a major role in helping to realize the SDGs. Two SDGs mention forests explicitly. SDG15, "Life on land", targets sustainable forest management. SDG6, "Clean water and sanitation", requests protection and restoration of forests in one of its targets. 14 of the 17 SDGs have forest-related indicators (Linser & Lier, 2020). The underlying data and information for these indicators, or parts of them, are based on the forest sector. They underline the cross-cutting nature of many forest-related indicators that extend beyond the forest sector, such as wood for energy or carbon indicators.

C&I for SFM processes

The forest sector pioneered the development and application of indicators to monitor progress against sustainability. In the 1990s, the indicator sets had already been developed for every world's region. As visible in Figure 2, by 2000, 171 countries were participating in 11 regional processes to develop C&I for SFM (Linser *et al.*, 2018b).

Today there are only six C&I for SFM processes, proactively coordinating and supporting their member countries (Linser *et al.*, 2018b):

- The International Tropical Timber Organization (ITTO) C&I for sustainable management of tropical forests (1986-ongoing).

- The Pan-European Forest Process on C&I for SFM (Forest Europe) (1990-ongoing).

- The MP on Criteria and Indicators for the Conservation and Sustainable Management of Temperate and Boreal Forests (1993-ongoing).

---

8   EuropaBON H2020 project: https://europabon.org/

9   100 EUROSTAT Sustainable Development Indicators: https://ec.europa.eu/eurostat/web/sdi/indicators

10 Global indicator framework for SDGs: https://unstats.un.org/sdgs/indicators/Global%20Indicator%20Framework%20after%202021%20refinement_Eng.pdf

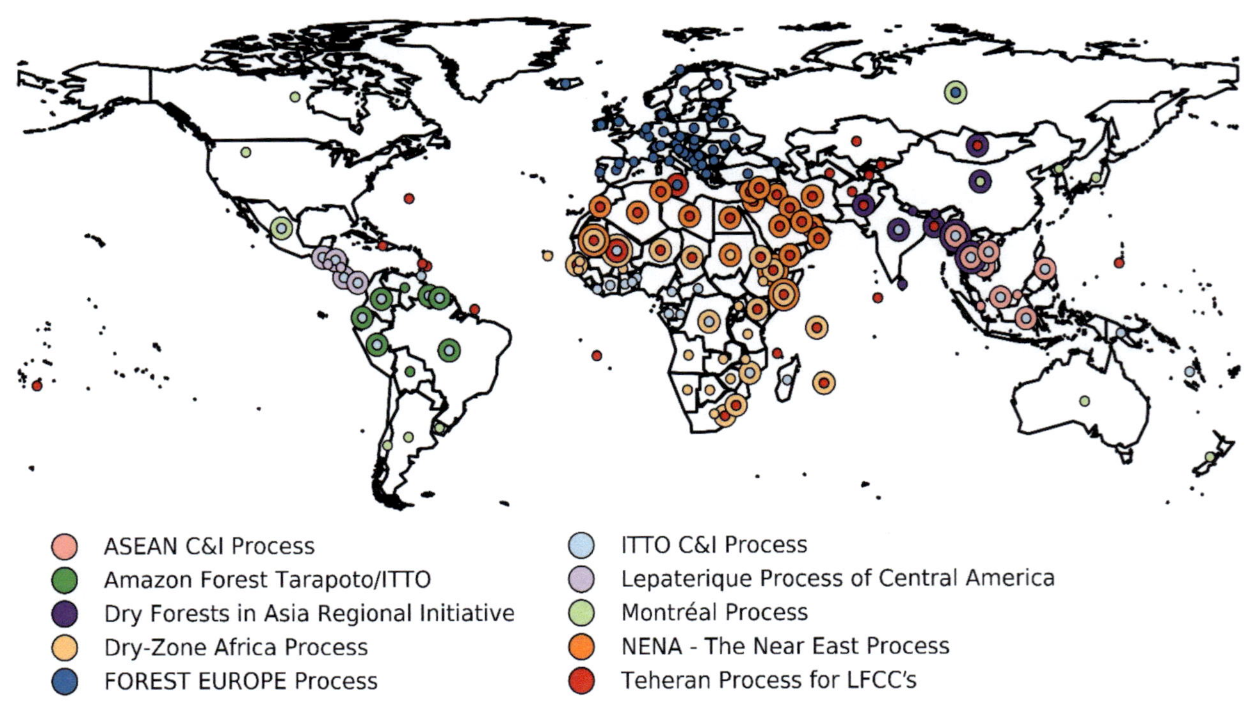

Source: Linser *et al.*, 2018b.

Note: A total of 171 countries were analysed. 52 countries participate in two processes. Six countries participate in three processes. Armenia, Azerbaijan, Guinea, Nigeria, North Korea, Paraguay and Uzbekistan do not participate in any of the listed processes. The Amazon Cooperation Treaty Organization (ACTO) is included in ITTO.

- The Amazon Cooperation Treaty Organization (ACTO) Tarapoto/ITTO Process on C&I for the sustainability of Amazon forests (1995-ongoing).

- The Association of Southeast Asian Nations (ASEAN) C&I for the sustainable management of tropical forests in Southeast Asia (1998-ongoing).

- The Low-Forest-Cover-Countries Process (LFCC) (2000-ongoing).

Partnership in data collection

Indicator-based forest and forestry data are a comprehensive reference and information framework on the current state of forests, related to the fulfilment of the ecological, economic and social functions of forests and their sustainable management.

The FAO Global Forest Resources Assessment is the main source of information on the state of the forests globally. It has collated and reported forest-related information regularly since 1948. In 2011, FAO introduced a new Collaborative Forest

Resources Questionnaire (CFRQ) partnership that consists of six organizations or regional and international processes: FAO, UNECE, Forest Europe, ITTO, the MP and the Observatory of the Central African Forests Commission. The CFRQ is the successful outcome of the joint commitment of these organizations and the C&I processes to streamline and harmonize forest-related data collection, easing the reporting burden. The remaining regional and international C&I processes are not part of the CFRQ due to being at different stages in their development, especially the availability of harmonized data. Joint data collection first took place in 2014, and was repeated in 2018, covering 88% of the global forest area in 103 countries.

To streamline the collection of comparable information which is relevant for all countries worldwide, the Collaborative Partnership on Forests developed the Global Core Set of Forest-related Indicators[11] - a selection of 21 forest-relevant key indicators to be measured at national level (FAO, 2018). These show global trends towards achieving the 2030 Agenda for Sustainable Development (including monitoring SDG

---

11 Global Core Set of Forest-related Indicators: http://www.fao.org/3/MW547EN/mw547en.pdf

Indicator 15.2.1 on SFM), the United Nations Strategic Plan for Forests, the UNFF Global Objectives of Forests and the obligations from the Rio Conventions. The set forms the basis for the country-wide analysis presented in the State of Europe's Forest 2020 Report[12] (Köhl *et al.*, 2020) as well as for defining the scope of INForest – a data and knowledge platform for forests in the UNECE region[13].

Benefits of having a national set of C&I for SFM

Many countries have developed national C&I sets, comprising some or all indicators from regional or international C&I processes, as well as indicators that are of importance nationally. A national C&I set for SFM takes account of national stakeholder values, common objectives, priorities and goals. It should form the basis for evidence-based policy, decision-making and communication, which will assist in:

- Defining SFM within a national context.

- Revealing the multi-functionality of forests.

- Preparing forest development and forest management plans.

- Monitoring, assessing and periodic reporting of the state of countries' forests and forest sector.

- Strengthening the development or revision of forest legislation, forest policy or national forest programmes and monitoring and assessing their implementation.

- Providing incentives for practical sustainable forest management.

- Encouraging dialogue and communication on key forest sector issues within the forest sector, between the forest and other sectors as well as with society.

- Demonstrating how forests benefit society.

The core user groups of national, indicator-based data and information are governmental organizations and authorities, such as forest policy, bioeconomy, environmental or climate institutions, as well as national accounting services, forest owners, forest owner interest groups, NGO's and the science community.

Guidelines for the development of national C&I for SFM

In 2019, UNECE and FAO produced Guidelines for the Development of a Criteria and Indicator Set for SFM[14] while supporting the development of national C&I sets for Armenia, Georgia, Kazakhstan, Kyrgyzstan and Uzbekistan as a basis for monitoring, reporting and assessing progress towards SFM and towards the SDGs (UNECE/FAO, 2019).

The Guidelines are universally applicable. They present a step-by-step approach to initiating a participatory consultative process to develop C&I for SFM. The Guidelines share concepts, definitions and tools and reference materials to support the process. The Guidelines feature a comprehensive list of global, international and regional C&I sets that countries can use to develop or improve their own national C&I sets, including the C&I sets of Forest Europe, the MP, the Low-Forest-Cover-Countries Process, ITTO and the FRA. The Guidelines identify information and tools to implement SFM at the national level, focusing on the identification of national indicators that are measurable, feasible, practicable and easily communicated.

Sustainability assessments with assigned targets

Nearly three decades after the Helsinki Ministerial Conference, where SFM[15] was first defined for pan-Europe, there are, as yet, no international agreed thresholds for the pan-European SFM C&I. Targets or thresholds for individual indicators have been developed, on an experimental basis, for the State of Europe's Forests Report 2011 (Forest Europe, 2011), for the Austrian C&I for SFM[16] (Linser, 2020) and in the SEMAFOR project[17] (UNECE/FAO, 2016).

SEMAFOR was initiated by the UNECE/FAO Team of Specialist on Monitoring SFM. It resulted in an innovative regional assessment method to measure objectively progress towards SFM in European countries, aiming to answer two questions: "What are the sustainabilty related areas of concern in a given country?" and "How are the areas of concern being addressed now?" The SEMAFOR concept is based on two major ideas:

---

12   State of Europe's Forest 2020 Report: https://www.researchgate.net/publication/348389865_State_of_Europe's_Forests_2020

13   INForest: https://forest-data.unece.org/

14   Guidelines for the Development of a Criteria and Indicator Set for SFM: https://www.unece.org/fileadmin/DAM/timber/publications/DP-73-ci-guidelines-en.pdf

15   Second Ministerial Conference on the Protection of Forests in Europe 16-17 June 1993, Helsinki/Finland - RESOLUTION H1 General Guidelines for the Sustainable Management of Forests in Europe: https://www.foresteurope.org/docs/MC/MC_helsinki_resolutionH1.pdf

16   Austrian C&I for SFM: https://www.researchgate.net/publication/347604457_Indikatoren_fur_nachhaltige_Waldbewirtschaftung_2020_Austrian_Indicators_for_Sustainable_Forest_Management_2020

17   SEMAFOR project: http://www.unece.org/index.php?id=45451

(1) using Pan-European indicators to assess progress towards SFM in European countries, setting common thresholds, and

(2) using the indicators to begin/conduct a dialogue with national experts who, for example, assess the recorded data in light of threats to SFM or policy measures being put in place to address identified issues.

It combines objective and transparent measurements with a modulated approach, which takes account of national circumstances, to produce credible and meaningful results, going beyond description to assessment.

Presently thresholds or targets assigned to the various indicators are increasingly sought for comprehensive sustainability assessments (Lier *et al.*, 2021; Linser *et al.*, 2018a; Onida, 2021; UNECE/FAO, 2019;). Future indicator revisions should address these needs.

Policy implications

The results of C&I information are helpful to define the scope of SFM and the topics that need to be monitored and assessed. Further, obtained information contributes to the revision of national forest strategies, programmes and assessment against the goals and targets included in national policy documents. C&I-based information might be used to formulate and assess progress towards quantitative targets set in forest-related strategies and provide evidence-based information to support new targets in forest-related regional strategies and action plans (e.g. EU Forest Strategy, ITTO Strategic Action Plan). This applies equally at the global level, where the indicators under SDG 15 measure progress towards SFM contributing to achieve the 2030 United Nations Agenda for Sustainable Development. The Global Core Set of Forest-related Indicators measures progress in implementing the International Arrangement on Forests, particularly the achievement of the UNFF Global Objectives of Forests.

C&I sets in general, and the Global Core Set in particular, have roles as "norm setters" and stimuli, informing governments of the data to be collected for every indicator of the set to meet their reporting obligations. The data that are collected and reported regularly for the Global Core Set are expected to lead to a voluntary de facto global minimum standard of information on forests and forestry that every country should meet.

The successes in developing forest-related indicators depends on much more than data availability. It requires ongoing political and institutional commitment, stewardship, a coordination unit, a clear derivation from political goals, broader communication instruments, capacity-building and linkages with official statistics and the approaches to sustainability taken by other sectors. It requires effective monitoring, analysis and reporting tools, harmonized terms and definitions and the means to assess sustainable forest management. It also needs action to modify policies and management where reports show that forest management is unsustainable.

The way forward

The forest sector is a global leader in developing and applying C&I. This lead has given the sector a head start on reporting SDG 15 forest-related indicators (FAO, 2017). C&I for SFM are increasingly adapted to address forest-related sustainable development issues across other sectors, such as bioeconomy or climate change. The continued commitment of countries, intergovernmental bodies and fora presents opportunities for more positive impact on global forest policy statements, regional and national forest strategies, development plans and other policy instruments. Together, these will strengthen progress towards SFM.

Best practice national C&I sets

The **Austrian** C&I for SFM set was developed in 2005 and has been revised several times to adapt to changing needs and emerging issues. The set contains 32 pan-European quantitative indicators as well as 33 additional indicators of national importance. The C&I set was adopted by the Austrian Forest Forum and is well integrated in national forest policymaking, as all indicators are directly related to the goals of the Austrian Forest Programme and the Austrian Forest Strategy 2020+. All data is presented in time series. For the indicator reports 2017 and 2020, each indicator contains agreed targets or thresholds as well as related assessments of the achievements, which makes this set unique in comparison to what is so far available in other countries. The report is written in German, but also contains in English: the introduction, summary, list of indicators, targets and thresholds. A selection of key indicators and related data and information is presented in separate leaflets available in several languages.

Please see: Austrian Federal Ministry of Agriculture, Regions and Tourism - Austrian Indicators for Sustainable Forest Management, 2020

Available at: https://info.bmlrt.gv.at/dam/jcr:2d25b3e7-8f0c-4556-8041 0c84f8741746/Indikatoren%20 f%C3%BCr%20nachhaltige%20Waldbewirtschaftung%202020.pdf

The **Australian** C&I for SFM set is based on the framework of the MP C&I for the Conservation and Management of Temperate and Boreal Forests. In 1998 the national-level MP Implementation Group for Australia adapted the 54 MP indicators to better suit reporting on Australia's unique forests. In 2006 the indicator set was reduced to 44 national indicators which have since been used as the basis for regular reports on a five-year interval. All 44 national indicators are aligned with the 54 MP indicators. The fifth report in the series, Australia's State of the Forests Report 2018, enables an efficient connection between state, national and international reporting processes. The report is driven through national processes such as reporting requirements for regional forest agreements and Australia's national forest policy. In turn, it provides data directly for international reporting obligations, including FRA or SDGs.

Please see: Australian Department of Agriculture and Water Resources – Australia's State of the Forests Report, 2018.

Available at: https://www.awe.gov.au/sites/default/files/abares/forestsaustralia/documents/sofr_2018/web%20 accessible%20pdfs/SOFR_2018_web.pdf

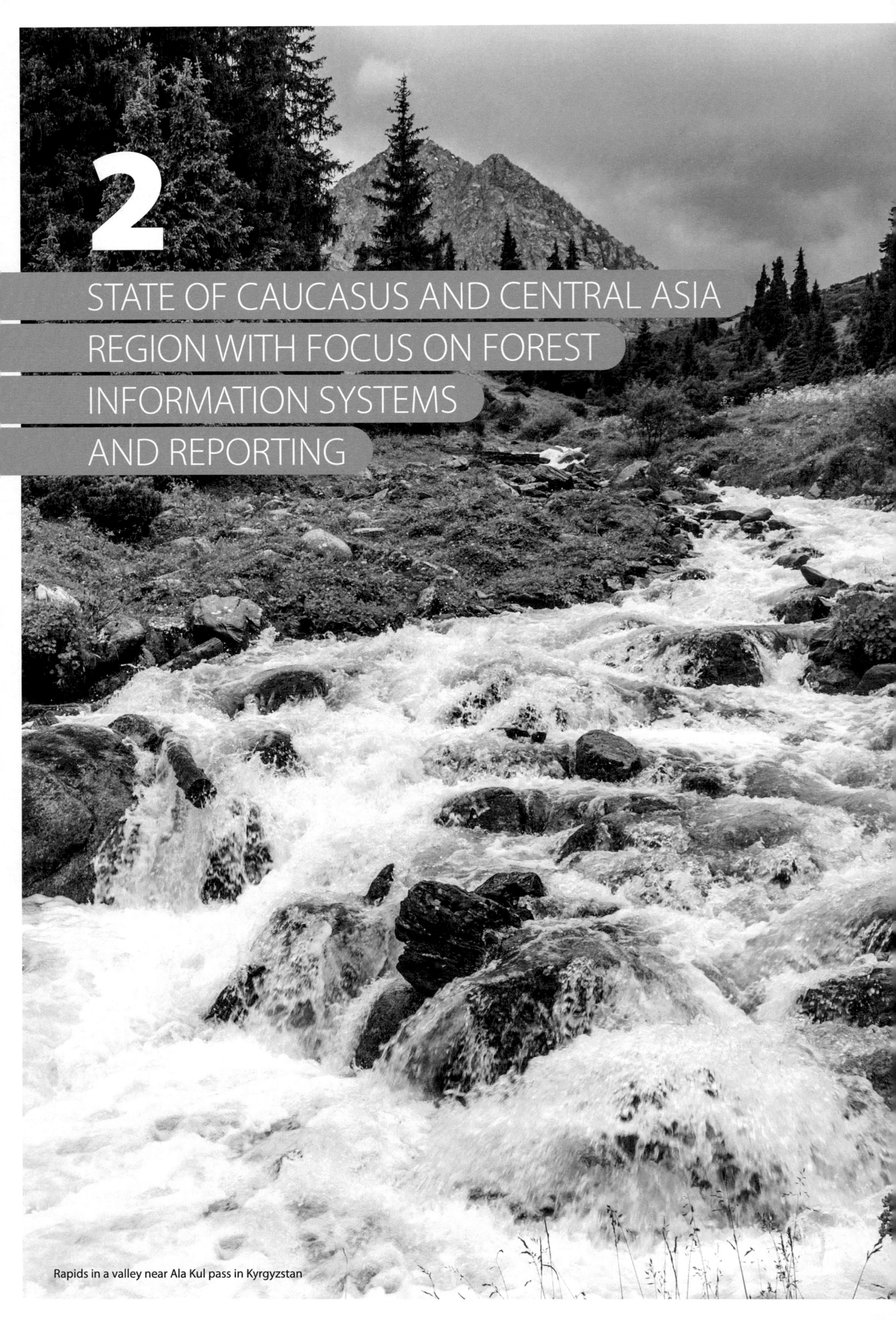

Rapids in a valley near Ala Kul pass in Kyrgyzstan

2. State of Caucasus and Central Asia region with Focus on Forest Information Systems and Reporting

The Caucasus and Central Asia (CCA) region covers an area of more than 420 million hectares at the centre of Eurasia, consisting of eight countries: Armenia, Azerbaijan, Georgia, Kazakhstan, Kyrgyzstan, Tajikistan, Turkmenistan and Uzbekistan. The countries gained independence after the collapse of the former Soviet Union in 1991. Agriculture is of paramount importance. It supports the livelihoods of a large majority of the population in rural areas. The sector suffers from insufficient financial and technology transfer arrangements and is characterized by small to medium farms with mono-cropping, low productivity and low income.

Forests occupy less than 7 per cent of the land area of the region, but play an important role in the overall ecosystem with rich biodiversity and valuable protective functions. There are many forest types and ecosystems, ranging from mountains, plains, flood plains, steppes, semi-deserts and deserts. Saxaul forests and shrubby vegetation occupy a sizeable proportion of forest land. Forests are crucial in preventing erosion in this highly mountainous and desert-prone region. Substantial areas of forests in the region are specifically devoted to biodiversity conservation. Forests are widely recognized for their contribution to rural economies, providing a wide range of wood and non-wood products. There is less widespread recognition of forests' ecological, economic and social functions and forest use is often unsustainable.

There are many similarities between the countries in terms of forest sector development. Most forests are State-owned and -managed. Few countries encourage or promote private forestry. With the exception of Georgia, most countries have limited forest cover. Forest management is constrained by limited resources, a shortage of qualified personnel, a lack of coordination and cooperation between sectors and low public awareness of forestry issues (UNECE/FAO, 2019a).

Existing forest ecosystems are vulnerable to the dry and sharply continental climate, desertification, uncontrolled fires, pests and diseases, as well as abiotic and biotic factors. Climate change effects worsens the situation in this highly sensitive environment. Deforestation and forest degradation are widespread, mainly as a consequence of overgrazing and illegal harvesting.

The dismantling of the Soviet Union disrupted many economic sectors, including the forest one. Many countries were not able to maintain their forest management planning system.

Several former Soviet Union countries lost the technical and financial resources to conduct regular forest inventories, leading to problems in systematic data collection and forest monitoring. Many forest statistics were outdated, based on old and mainly local reports. Different reporting structures and incomplete coverage have made it difficult to aggregate data to provide meaningful and reliable information about forests at the national level.

However, some signs of improvement have been observed owing to the introduction of projects to advance forest management planning systems and to conduct national forestry inventories. Remote sensing, using GIS technology, has become more affordable. Digital infrastructure that could support efforts to design forest information systems exists now in several countries. Organizations such as FAO and UNECE, and donor-funded projects have accelerated work to support improved means for monitoring, storing and analysing data and information. Despite promising progress, development is slow, primarily because of the lack of qualified staff. Regrettably, many trained, skilled and experienced staff have left the forest sector for more attractive jobs elsewhere. This, in addition to the unavailability of funding, is a major constraint to improving forest monitoring, data collection and reporting.

In the decade following the 1993 MCPFE Helsinki Conference, work on refining the meaning and practice of sustainable forest management progressed; later, this work also included the elaboration of related criteria and indicators. The turmoil that followed the collapse of the Soviet Union affected the ability of most of the CCA countries to participate in the respective processes. Georgia is the only CCA country that participates in the Forest Europe process. Kyrgyzstan is a member of the Near East process but without significant active involvement. Consequently, no CCA country had applied the C&I for SFM sets of the various processes nor developed their own national sets of criteria and indicators for sustainable forest management. Balanced, credible and objective reporting structures are absent from almost all CCA countries.

The next section summarizes the current situation in the five project countries.

Armenia

Forest extends to 328,470 ha[18], around 11 per cent of the land area. Illegal logging is the main cause of forest degradation. All forests are State-owned. The State-Non-Profit-Organization "Hayantar SNCO" is responsible for the management of 75 per cent of forests; one-quarter is managed by the Bioresources Management Agency of the Ministry of Environment. Forest ecosystems, mostly occurring in south and north-east Armenia, play a crucial role in preventing environmental degradation.

---

18   Global FRA 2020 country page of Armenia: http://www.fao.org/3/ca9966en/ca9966en.pdf

More than two-thirds of the forests are broadleaved. Despite having such an important role in preserving biodiversity and providing valuable ecosystem services, the forest sector's economic contribution to Armenia's economy is minor.

Forest monitoring and information systems are poor. Recent structural changes in the way forestry is organized hold promise of improvement, but currently the country struggles with the provision of reliable information on forest management and forest conditions. A lack of financial capacity and qualified personnel are the primary constraints.

Armenia participated both in FRA 2015[19] and FRA 2020, reporting a limited amount of the requested information. They also contributed limited data to the Joint Wood Energy Enquiry[20], and responded to the UNECE/FAO Joint Forest Sector Questionnaire 2022.

Georgia

Forests extend to 2,822,400 ha[21], or 41 per cent of the land area, a figure that has remained stable since 2005. All forest land is publicly owned through a State Forest Fund[22] and the great majority is managed by the National Forestry Agency. For some forests long-term harvesting licences were issued during 2007-2011.

Most forests are of natural origin, located in mountainous areas and mainly provide protective functions. Biodiversity conservation is one of the main management objectives even outside of protected forest areas. Forestry's contribution to the national economy is minor but could be increased by better utilization of large areas of forest.

The management plans of the State Forest Fund are the basic sources of data for forest monitoring. Inventories were reintroduced in 2013 and are carried out through ground and aerial surveys using orthophotography. Sample plot measurements support monitoring of some sections of forests. There is no comprehensive digital mapping system with functional zoning used for forestry.

Georgia participated both in FRA 2015 and FRA 2020, responded to the UNECE/FAO Joint Forest Sector Questionnaire 2022, but did not contribute to the Joint Wood Energy Enquiry. Georgia reports forest-related information to FAO, UNCBD, UNFCCC and UNCCD. Georgia is the only project country that participates in Forest Europe's regional C&I for SFM process and provided indicator-based data and information for the Joint UNECE/FAO/Forest Europe pan-European reporting[23].

The main constraints to improve the forest information systems are the limited capacity of forest-related institutions and lacking forest stakeholder engagement.

A new forest legislation (forest code[24]) was ratified by parliament in spring 2020 which ensures sustainable forest management and regular indicator- based inventories.

Kazakhstan

The area of the publicly owned Forest Fund covers over 30 million ha of land, but only 3,454,680 ha[25] are classified as forest by the international definition (crown cover over 10 per cent); 9.5 million ha are "other wooded land" (crown cover between 5 and 10 per cent). The total of "forest and other wooded land" covers 4.7 per cent of the total land area. Half of the Forest Fund land is covered by saxaul trees and a quarter by other bushy species. These figures have remained stable since 2005. Almost three-quarters of the forest area is managed by local authorities (akimats) and the other quarter by the Forestry and Wildlife Committee of the Ministry of Ecology, Geology and Natural Resources. Recent national forestry policy has supported developing private forestry and establishing green belts around cities as well as introducing new technologies to protect forests from fires, pests and diseases. Forests have an important protective role in preventing environmental degradation, especially soil erosion and desertification. Forest programmes and action plans are rather short-term in outlook. Addressing this issue, in 2021, the UNECE/FAO Forestry and Timber Section helped Kazakhstan to develop its master plan for forestry.

An information system, called SOLI_N, has been designed for the monitoring of forests, and is also used for processing forest inventory data. There are biodiversity information systems designed for four pilot protected areas.

---

19 Global FRA 2015 country report of Armenia: http://www.fao.org/3/a-az154e.pdf

20 Joint Wood Energy Enquiry: https://www.unece.org/forests/jwee.html

21 Global FRA 2020 country page of Georgia: http://www.fao.org/3/cb0001en/cb0001en.pdf

22 State Forest Fund is a tenure category common to all former Soviet Union countries. In general, the State Forest Fund refers to all forests, forested and non-forested areas owned or administered by the State forestry authorities.

23 Joint pan-European dataset: https://fra-data.fao.org/GEO/panEuropean/home/

24 Forest Code of Georgia (No. 5949-SS of 2020): http://extwprlegs1.fao.org/docs/pdf/geo196014ENG.pdf

25 Global FRA 2020 country page of Kazakhstan: https://fra-platform.herokuapp.com/KAZ/assessment/fra2020/extentOfForest/

Kazakhstan did not participate in FRA 2015, nor the Joint Wood Energy Enquiry, but responded to the FRA 2020 questionnaire[26].

Kyrgyzstan

The publicly owned forests cover 1,315.38 ha[27] or about 8 per cent of the land area, based on the Global FRA 2020 report. The local level forest administrations (leskhoz) manage forests with oversight from the Division of Forest Ecosystems. There are four main forest types: spruce forests in the western and central areas; walnut forests in the south; tugai forests along riversides; and juniper forests growing all over the country. Forests are important in preventing environmental degradation. Grazing and firewood collection are the main causes of forest degradation, together with illegal logging, which is in a downward trend. Forests make an insignificant contribution to Kyrgyzstan's national GDP.

There is no integrated database for forest-related information. Instead, data are maintained in separate databases held within different units. For reporting purposes, data are compiled from these separate databases and complemented with information from other sources. Kyrgyzstan participated both in FRA 2015 and FRA 2020 with data of differentiated quality. It responded to the UNECE/FAO Joint Forest Sector Questionnaire (2022) but did not contribute to the Joint Wood Energy Enquiry.

Uzbekistan

Forests cover 3,689.66 ha[28] or about 7 per cent of the land area and this figure is increasing. The State Committee on Forestry manages all forest. Forests provide a significant protective function, playing an important role in combating desertification and preventing erosion, as well as protecting irrigated agricultural land and pastures from degradation. There are three main forest types in Uzbekistan: Saxaul in the desert regions, mountain forests including juniper in the south and east, and tugai riverine forests. Forests and forestry have a significant impact on other sectors of the national economy, such as agriculture, livestock and water conservation. Their contribution to national GDP is minor. Overgrazing, drought and salinization are the main problems for sustainable forest management in Uzbekistan.

Inadequate financial resources, the absence of modern information systems and equipment constrain data collection and forest monitoring. Uzbekistan reports forest-related information to FAO, CBD, UNFCCC and UNCCD. It participated both in FRA 2015 and FRA 2020. It did not respond to the

UNECE/FAO Joint Forest Sector Questionnaire (2022), nor the Joint Wood Energy Enquiry.

---

26   Global FRA 2020 country page of Kyrgyzstan: http://www.fao.org/3/cb0018en/cb0018en.pdf

27   Global FRA 2020 report of Kyrgyzstan: http://www.fao.org/3/cb0020en/cb0020en.pdf

28   Global FRA 2020 country page of Uzbekistan: http://www.fao.org/3/cb0087en/cb0087en.pdf

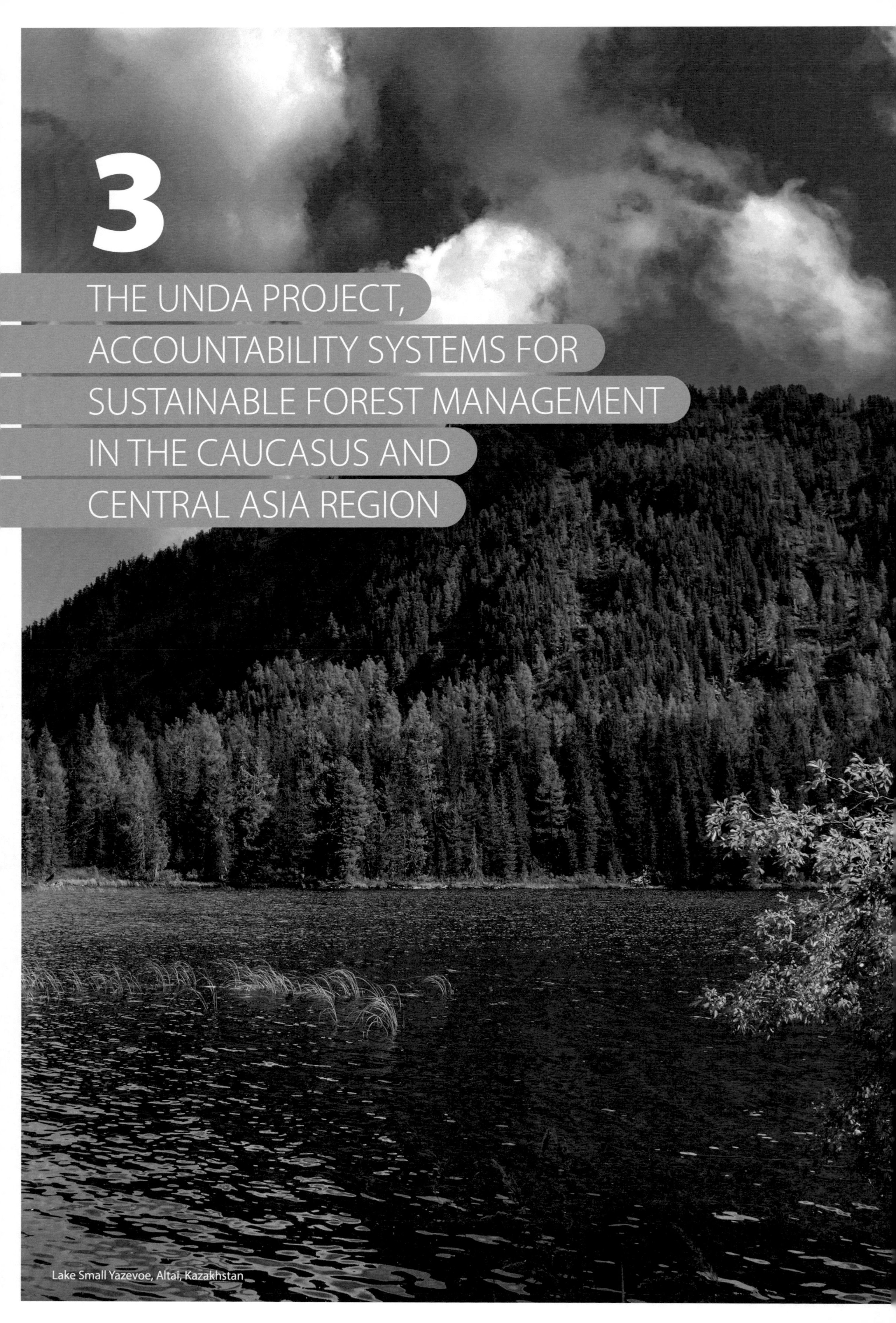

Lake Small Yazevoe, Altai, Kazakhstan

3. The UNDA Project, Accountability systems for sustainable forest management in the Caucasus and Central Asia region

The UNDA Project, "Accountability systems for sustainable forest management in the Caucasus and Central Asia" was implemented in five countries: Armenia; Georgia; Kazakhstan; Kyrgyzstan; and Uzbekistan, supporting them to develop national C&I for SFM as well as related monitoring, reporting or accountability systems.

An aim of the project was to support countries in developing information-based forest policy- and decision-making systems and to encourage their participation in international forest-related processes. The design provided technical assistance to enable countries to monitor, assess and report their progress towards SFM.

It provided the knowledge and necessary skills through training materials and advisory services that would allow countries to define and implement national C&I for SFM.

Gap analysis

A preliminary analysis showed that countries expected the project would help to:

- assist forest institutions to understand the multi-functionality of forests

- identify the information necessary to influence policy processes

- identify how the needs and challenges of data collection could be met

- define national C&I for SFM as a basis for developing a comprehensive monitoring system

- obtain examples of best-practice forest monitoring systems

- increase the visibility of the forest sector and set up cooperation with national agencies and stakeholders

- improve the participation of those five countries in international reporting

Project intentions

The basic idea of the project was that proper monitoring, assessment and accountability systems would improve the understanding of the status of forest management in the project countries. Furthermore, the project aimed to help them to identify what might need to be done to improve SFM and to take necessary action. The project focused on defining the scope and information needed, gaps in data collection and developing national C&I for SFM. It addressed officials, forestry-related ministries and institutions.

Project facilitation

The project was managed by the Joint UNECE/FAO Forestry and Timber Section. Experts from Austria, Czech Republic, Estonia, Germany, Iran, Norway, Poland the Russian Federation, Slovakia, and Turkey, together with international organizations such as, FAO and UNECE contributed through presentations, advice, panel discussions and the exchange of views. The project shared best practice from other countries, introduced sets of C&I for SFM of various intergovernmental processes along with studies such as SEMAFOR (UNECE/FAO, 2016) and released tailored materials such as the "Guidelines for the Development of a Criteria and Indicator Set for SFM" (UNECE/FAO, 2019b).

First phase of implementation

A number of coaching workshops provided the main framework for the project's implementation. They served as a platform to analyse current national conditions and to initiate preparatory work to define national C&I for SFM.

Commonalities

There were many common factors among countries, including: the effect of the Soviet Union's collapse; the lack of robust forest policies and financial resources; weak institutions, disrupted forest management and monitoring systems, illegal logging and degradation; and public forest ownership.

National priorities

Most of the project countries put great emphasis on the protection that their forests provide to the soil, water and biodiversity resources. Georgia also placed considerable emphasis on the sustainable production of goods and services from forests. The low-forest-cover countries prioritized expanding their forest area. In addition, the project countries mentioned that rehabilitation and restoration of forest areas was a high priority. Enhancing rural development and agroforestry as well as attracting private sector investment were also mentioned as areas of high interest. The project's primary achievement was emphasizing that all these issues should be considered in a comprehensive way.

From a technical point of view, many issues in developing sound C&I for SFM were clarified. Relevance to national conditions was seen as the most important factor in this development. Early drafts contained some indicators under nationally irrelevant criteria, derived from more general intergovernmental C&I for SFM sets, but participants increasingly focused on their own needs and finally derived criteria and indicators of particular national importance, including those for reporting obligations towards FRA, Global Core Set of Forest-related Indicators, Forest Europe and others.

Sustainability as a starting point for all considerations

Sustainable forest management was at the heart of all discussions. SFM considers all the benefits that forests offer. Where improvements in management are needed, SFM criteria can be used module by module in a logical and integrated way. Implementing quantitative and qualitative C&I for SFM will give prioritized guidance for policy and strategy development, provided that all stakeholders have agreed to them. This could pave the road towards feasible and effective projects or programmes, including NFPs.

At the outset, most workshop participants believed that it would be impossible to end up with a comprehensive forest monitoring owing to limited resources. In discussions, participants recognized that there was no universal C&I based sustainable forest management system, even in those countries where the development of C&I for SFM is advanced. All countries faced challenges in developing C&I-based sustainable forest management. Countries in the CCA can benefit from international experience of countries that have already developed and implemented their C&I and made efforts to adapt their C&I-based forest management in practical and affordable ways. Countries will need further strong motivation, determination and foresight to develop the forest sector further, coupled with timely and deliberate action.

Applicability, completeness, verification and usefulness

Applicability was another important factor. To fulfil international reporting obligations, countries accepted that it might be necessary to include data indicators that they were not yet able to collect and monitor, even if this might initially risk less comprehensive national C&I for SFM. The entire implementation of a national C&I system is time and resource consuming. This might also cause "data availability bias", as some countries may not be able to provide data for the next reporting periods.

It is essential to verify the data, as they will be used to inform decision making. Unverified data might lead to incorrect conclusions. Those participants working in science and research pointed to the sensitivity of using verified data for indicators. Indicators usually address policymakers, affiliates from academia and a wide range of stakeholders. The ways of communicating with target audiences must be considered

when defining and designing indicators. The coaching workshops succeeded in clarifying the concept of C&I for SFM, through examining international best practice. This showed convincingly how sound monitoring, assessment and reporting of C&I for SFM could trigger sustainable forest management. Reviewing C&I from intergovernmental processes, using a scoring technique, helped to identify those indicators which might be of national relevance to CCA countries. Countries agreed to structure the criteria in compliance with the seven thematic elements of SFM[29], as approved by the United Nations General Assembly (UN, 2007a).

Dedication

The five countries shared their first drafts of national C&I for SFM at an interim workshop, held from 20-23 February 2018 in Tbilisi. The discussions that followed helped to improve national C&I for SFM and guided future planned work. All five countries showed a clear interest in setting recommendations that would enhance national sets of C&I and guide better methods for collecting data. A rich set of presentations induced further discussion and thinking about the final shape of national sets. Presentations about two publications (Linser *et al.* 2018 a and b) in particular added much by providing insights into the C&I for SFM processes.

Second phase of implementation

Subsequent national workshops made substantial progress in finalizing draft national C&I, based on a common understanding of SFM. Participants, representing various forest sectors' stakeholders, characterized the essential components of forestry in developing national C&I for SFM. The next step was to work out how to measure progress against each component, and then to find feasible ways to consolidate the information. National and international experts helped to shape the criteria for SFM; subsequently the participants assessed the relevance, availability and feasibility of potential indicators.

Different national approaches

Considering the latest developments in remote sensing and GIS technology which signalled a higher feasibility to collect more information about forests, **Armenia** greatly improved its preliminary set of C&I for SFM. The seven criteria aligned mainly with the ones of the Forest Europe process[30] and comprised a total of 43 indicators. The indicators consider reporting obligations towards FRA and the Global Core Set of Indicators. Armenia established a particular working group to finalize its national set of C&I for SFM.

---

29   UN Thematic Elements of SFM: http://www.fao.org/forestry/ci/16609/en/

30   Forest Europe Criteria for SFM: https://foresteurope.org/sfm-criteria-indicators/

Being a member of the Forest Europe process, **Georgia** – from the very beginning – oriented the development of their national C&I on the pan-European C&I for SFM. A total of 14 criteria and 43 indicators and 37 sub-indicators were identified. Georgia prepared a rich set of indicators covering more than three quarters of the pan-European indicators as well as multitude of criteria and indicators of particular national importance. Carbon stock became a stand-alone criterion.

Furthermore, the set contains qualitative indicators on stakeholder participation and dissemination of information on SFM.

The new forest code, which was approved by the parliament in spring 2020, strongly supports the national C&I for SFM implementation, providing capacity-building opportunities and means for improving data accessibility.

Kazakhstan followed the approach of the Montréal Process Working Group on Criteria and Indicators for the Conservation and Sustainable Management of Temperate and Boreal Forests. The preliminary national C&I for SFM were discussed and agreed by various stakeholders, including those representing national regions, with the view of applying the set as a tool also at the regional level. The final set consisted of four criteria and 13 indicators. The chosen criteria covered the main aspects of major national interest and focus on conservation of biodiversity, maintenance of the productive capacity, forest protection and socio-economic benefits. While Kazakhstan was facing the challenge of establishing a first monitoring and reporting system, the related indicators are sufficient for reporting about sustainable forest management, even though the number of indicators is small.

Kyrgyzstan implemented a number of reforms recently, including introducing joint forest management schemes. Work is under way to update the forest code and prepare a national action plan for forestry. The final set of Kyrgyzstan's C&I for SFM embeds six criteria with 54 indicators, including 4 sub-indicators. The structure follows mainly the Forest Europe approach with criteria focusing on ecosystem conditions, biodiversity, productivity, the socio-economic importance of the sector, the social status of the workforce and with well elaborated qualitative indicators including for the political, legislative and institutional framework for SFM.

In **Uzbekistan**, the need to develop C&I for SFM has been addressed at the presidential level and this has generated momentum. Draft national C&I for SFM were prepared at local workshops organized by the State Committee on Forestry. Based on expert comments and proposals the set was improved. The national C&I for SFM set comprises seven criteria, 21 quantitative and seven qualitative indicators, one under each criterion, following the Forest Europe approach. Forest management planning was designated as a stand-alone criterion with some issues of national importance to be touched in respective indicators. The C&I for SFM set will be declared as part of an official resolution.

Intergovernmental and national indicators

Most countries based their preliminary sets of C&I for SFM on regional and international processes. Intensive discussions led to more and country-specific indicators next to those from intergovernmental sets, as countries included indicators of particular national importance in their final sets.

Commonalities

Common criteria among all countries were the maintenance of forest resources and the protection of biodiversity.

The area of FOWL characterized by various parameters such as type, age structure, naturalness, status (protective, productive or degraded) and functions exists in all national C&I for SFM sets with slightly different syntaxes but still suitable for the respective international reporting obligations. Some of the indicators are envisaged to monitor changes over time which could be used as assessment parameters (as defined in the SEMAFOR study, UNECE/FAO, 2016) but most of them are context parameters that describe certain conditions. Given the fact that most countries have no time series data for forest resources, it might not be possible to make an indicator-based assessment of the progress towards sustainability within the nearest period.

Biodiversity is highly valued across the CCA region but identifying biodiversity indicators is hindered by a lack of national surveys or inventories focusing on biodiversity issues. There are studies in some parts of the 5 countries, but little data and information exists at the national level. Monitoring biodiversity is a problem faced by many countries worldwide. Indicators such as species diversity, endemic species, threatened species, introduced species and invasive species are common indicators, as there is a high political and stakeholder interest, but data validity and reliability remain low as the respective monitoring is time and resource extensive and requires expert knowledge.

Importance of forest health and vitality

Under a criterion focusing on forest health and vitality, all countries included indicators on the area of forest damaged by various agents such as fire, drought, pests and diseases or overgrazing. Some stakeholders commented that silvicultural factors were often neglected in the regional or international sets of indicators for SFM. Silvicultural practices can affect the health and vitality of forests. With this in mind, some countries added indicators such as the size of regenerated forest areas, size of forest pastures, seeding, planting, afforestation, forest roads (accessibility) and fire protection strips next to permissions for grazing.

Indicators on productivity

Annual wood production and NWFP are most often used as a measure of productivity. Most stakeholders believed that key information should be provided on the amount and value of the goods and services derived from forests. Views on whether to include illegally harvested areas or amounts of wood varied. The question arose whether illegally harvested wood could be traced and recorded. Some countries considered it important to make an attempt to include some measure of illegal harvesting to give an idea about the trend of illegal wood removals from forests.

Focus on indicators on protected forest areas

The protective function of forests in the CCA countries is a major benefit. There was general recognition that all vital forests protect soil and water. However, quantifying that benefit is difficult or impossible with the present preconditions. There are some forest areas that have been designated specifically for soil and water protection. There was concern that limiting any measure of the protective function to only such designated areas would fail to reflect the true magnitude of the protective function of the forests and may well result in a significant undervaluation of those benefits. Some countries included a criterion on protection in their national C&I for SFM sets, containing indicators of forest areas managed specifically to protect soils, water and forests that are located in watersheds.

Multiple socio-economic issues covered by indicators

The criterion covering socio-economic benefits led to lengthy and intensive discussions. The 5 countries participating in the project have developed a rich set of indicators related to issues such as the value and consumption of wood and NWFP; forestry budgets and investments; export and import of forest products; the contribution to GDP, employment, health and safety of workers; and the contribution to rural livelihoods. Views differed on which indicators to include within the socio-economic criterion. As an example, wood production was an indicator within the "productive" criterion of some countries but was included within the socio-economic criterion in some other countries. It was agreed that, within the "productive" criterion, the focus would be the volumes of wood produced, whereas within the socio-economic criterion, the focus relates to the market value of the timber.

Qualitative indicators on policies, institutions and instruments

Some countries have also included a criterion on legal, policy and institutional frameworks with qualitative (descriptive) indicators related to legislation, institutions, policies, programmes and plans as well as science and research. Some countries covered respective indicators under the socio-economic criterion, and some followed the Forest Europe approach by placing "policies, institutions and instruments" as a respective indicator under each criterion.

Further necessities after indicator development

Some countries have been making progress in improving data collection systems and forest management planning, for example through various international projects. In general, all five countries acknowledged the need to expand their ability to undertake forest inventory and monitoring. While data obtained from the above-mentioned projects and from old inventories, management plans and similar sources could not provide sufficient information for SFM and the international reporting obligations, the present project paved the way to update data and broaden the coverage of forest inventories in accordance with the needs articulated by stakeholders.

Overall Assessment

The five countries of the project have made considerable progress in developing national C&I for SFM.

The process has encouraged setting up fora allowing participation of international experts, contributions from consultants, NGOs and other stakeholders, and the active involvement of personnel from national ministerial forestry and environment departments and forestry or environment agencies. This has resulted in the participatory elaboration of broadly acknowledged C&I for SFM sets in every target country.

Assistance towards self-determining C&I development

Countries were free to develop their own C&I for SFM sets and implementation models. The various stakeholders acknowledged that in order to design C&I that best reflect the state of forestry and forest management and that influence policy processes, they need to grasp the multifunctionality of forests. Presentations on the C&I for SFM development and implementations from various countries and intergovernmental processes, demonstrations of best cases, failures, problems and challenges have all helped in setting the scene in the minds of the participants. Stimulated by these inputs and with the help of project teams, countries drafted plans for further steps.

National reports show that countries worked effectively in between workshops, building links and cooperation with relevant institutions and stakeholders. Following feedback from national stakeholders and guidance of experts during and after workshops, all five countries finalized their national sets of C&I for SFM.

Technical challenges of implementation

All five countries faced challenges of insufficient funding and a shortage of human and technical capacities. It includes in particular a lack of professional and highly qualified technical staff for the implementation of SFM and its monitoring. Furthermore, the circumstances are framed by deficient public and private equipment.

These problems limited their capacities to: protect forests from illegal use, logging and grazing; ensure that the impacts of logging are kept as low as reasonably practical; restore degraded forest territories; and ensure that tending operations are carried out at the appropriate time. The lack of transport and communication vehicles hampered their abilities to guard forest territories. Further support was also needed for improving methods of operating forest nurseries and for raising quality and productivity in the cultivation of seedlings and saplings, in both nurseries and arboreta.

As the project progressed, it was increasingly internalized, that the forest sector institutions needed to be strengthened, by allocating sufficient resources (financial, technical and human) from the central budget and external sources to achieve the objectives stated in the first phase of implementation, including the improvements in administrative and managerial structures and processes. The local level forest administrations (leskhoz) needed support to update the technical means (computer, internet, communication, etc.) to conduct work with the general population on the importance of forest resource conservation and to allocate funding for biotechnical activities. These needs were also reflected by some countries in the proposals for indicators focused on professional organizations and well-educated technical staff for the implementation of SFM.

The participatory workshops organized within the project contributed also to the introduction of advanced scientific and technical achievements in the forest industry. These workshops helped to share information about national and international grants to the forest industry for the renewal of the material and technical base or the establishment of wood-based industries to enhance their added value.

Countries were also acquainted with the regional C&I processes relevant to the subregion. Regional C&I sets and related material were shared with project countries for methodological and technical support in developing their national sets.

Countries were also informed about earth observation-based remote sensing, which gains increasing importance for obtaining comparable data and information - for instance for the Global FRA (FAO, 2020) and Global Core Set of Forest-related Indicators (FAO, 2018). The factsheets of all countries also contain references to earth observation-based data sources.

Policy briefs to support awareness-raising and implementation

C&I for SFM are an increasingly common policy tool to implement sustainable management of forests and monitor progress. They are crucial in defining related specific targets for improving monitoring, reporting and assessment of key aspects of SFM.

However, there is a lack of knowledge among policymakers and decision makers on the use of C&I for various aspects of forests and forestry. Therefore, the Joint UNECE/FAO Forestry and Timber Section, together with specialists on monitoring SFM, developed the five policy briefs about various important aspects of C&I for SFM applications, such as:

- Criteria and indicators – a universal policy tool for Sustainable Forest Management
- Criteria and Indicators and National Forest Inventory – a tool for decision making
- Criteria and Indicators and Information Systems – a tool for better forest policy and management
- Criteria and indicators-based international Monitoring, Assessment and Reporting
- Criteria and indicators for forest-related communication

The full text of policy briefs can be found in chapters 2 and 5 of this publication.

4

INDICATORS, TARGETS AND THRESHOLDS IN NATIONAL CRITERIA AND INDICATORS FOR SUSTAINABLE FOREST MANAGEMENT

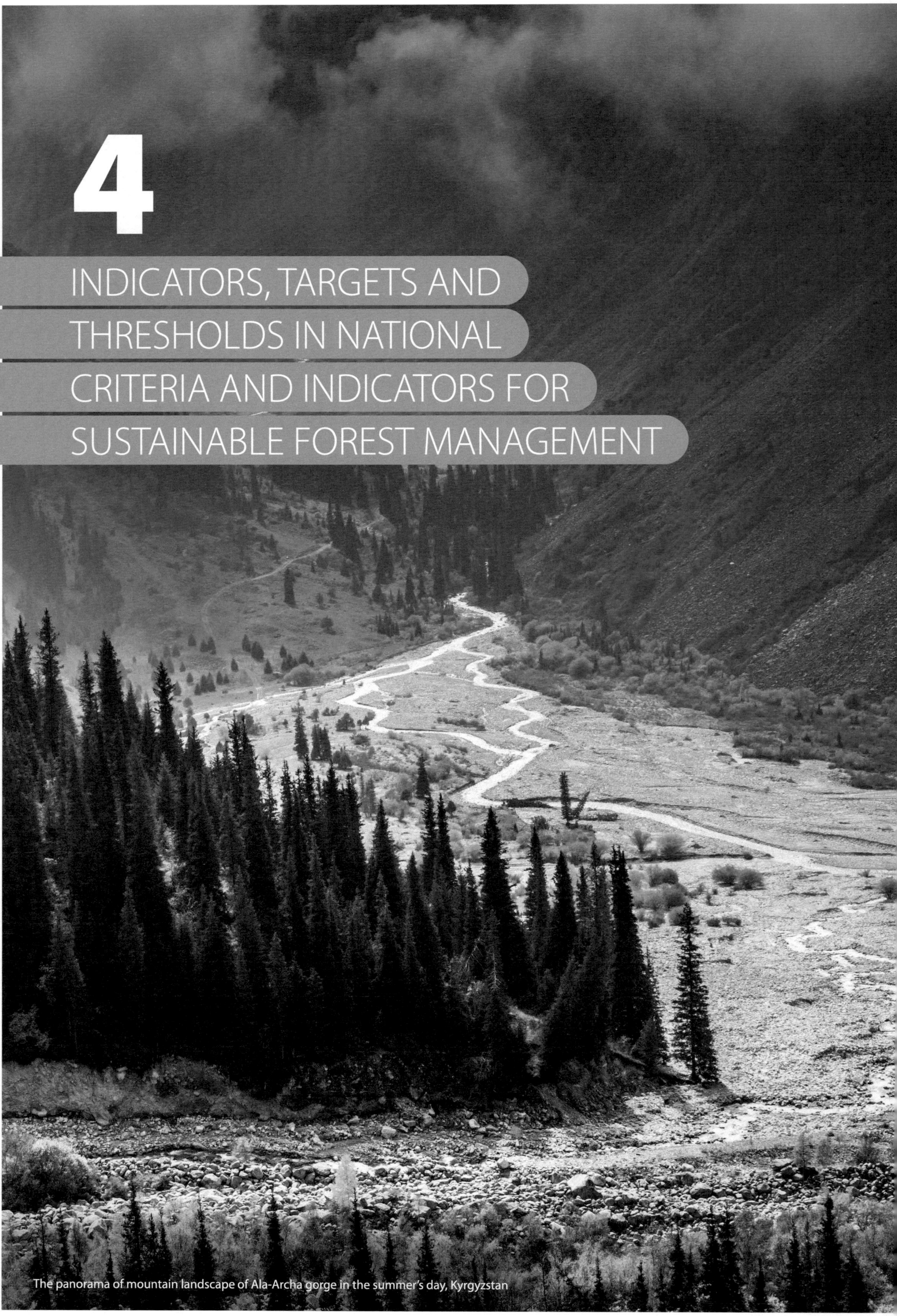

The panorama of mountain landscape of Ala-Archa gorge in the summer's day, Kyrgyzstan

4. Indicators, Targets and Thresholds in National Criteria and Indicators for Sustainable Forest Management

The sets of C&I for SFM for the CCA countries, reflect different types of indicators. Most of the indicators have assigned targets or thresholds. It is expected to have repeated inventories or monitoring activities, so that a respective sustainability assessment of the forest management can be based on data available in timelines.

The experimental pilot study, SEMAFOR, provides helpful guidance for the effective assessment of C&I for SFM (UNECE, 2016). The study is based on pan-European experiences of implementing C&I for SFM. It set out, *"to combine objective and transparent measurement with a modulated approach which takes account of national circumstances, to produce a result which is credible and meaningful, going beyond description to assessment"*. The study underlines the importance of a reporting structure that is useful to policymakers. It highlights internationally agreed targets and thresholds that can be used for deciding corrective action to be taken within the forest sector or by others. Thresholds act as flags, signalling whether more information may be needed to clarify specific issues, particularly when an agreed threshold has been exceeded.

Context, assessment and background indicators

It is not possible to assign targets or thresholds for every parameter of an indicator. Parameters fall into three categories: context, assessment or background. For any given indicator, a **context** parameter describes the country situation. **Assessment** parameters provide information for assessing the sustainability of forest management for a given indicator and do have target or threshold values. **Background** parameters are those for which it is difficult to provide a reliable description or assessment of sustainable forest management without additional information.

An example may help in clarifying these different categories of parameters. For the "forest area" indicator, the proportion of forest in relation to the total land area is a context parameter. It is not possible to assess SFM based on only the forest area at a given time. However, using this figure as a baseline puts the assessment parameter in context and allows the comprehensive assessment of annual changes. The threshold for this example could be "any negative change" and a target would be "to increase the forest area". "Age structure" is an example of a background parameter as it is difficult to

conclude on this parameter without additional information about functions assigned to assessed forests.

Development of factsheets

Factsheets for C&I could help to guide the monitoring, reporting and assessment. All five countries elaborated factsheets providing detailed background information on the selected indicators. These factsheets contain: the reference of the indicator to the respective criteria, information on the full name of the indicators and sub-indicators; a rationale why monitoring, assessing and reporting a particular indicator is of national importance; data sources; measurement units; periodicity of data availability, targets and/or thresholds; institutions which will collect, manage and use the data; references to international reporting obligations; and definitions of key terms. The detailed elaboration of the factsheets led to a further revision of the indicators, as this made it obvious how the indicators should be collected and if this would be feasible.

Key indicators for communication

For communication purposes, the countries discussed selecting a smaller set of key or headline indicators, in light of those indicators which are also part of the Global Core Set of Forest-related Indicators[31]. The indicators are based on the seven thematic elements approved by the United Nations General Assembly.

The focus of the selected indicators is presented in the next paragraphs per criteria which have the same content, even if the names differed slightly in the five countries.

4.1 Maintenance or Enhancement of the Extent of Forest Resources

The area and biomass of FOWL are the core of this criterion. Forest management plans, national forest inventories and increasingly, remote sensing, provide the source data. If possible, it is broken down by forest availability for wood supply, forest type, age and diameter classes. Management plans and/or forest inventories for most of the target countries are either outdated or may not cover all forest areas. Countries are unlikely, therefore, to be able to provide data about changes in area or growing stock at the first assessment period (first national report based on C&I for SFM). Even when forest management planning systems have been established, it will be some time before management plans cover the entire forest area. In the short-term, at least, indicators for this criterion are likely to remain context parameters.

---

31   Global Core Set of Forest-related Indicators: http://www.fao.org/3/MW547EN/mw547en.pdf

Key indicators are:

1. Area of FOWL
2. Growing stock
3. Carbon balance

The area of FOWL is among the most subdivided indicators. It is recommended that parameters are restricted to the distribution of FOWL (with forest separated from other wooded land), by forest type (conifer, broadleaved or mixed), and by age or diameter/development class.

The FAO definition of forest sometimes causes difficulty in assigning bush forest in CCA countries. Bush forest is a key element of the forest ecosystem in CCA countries and must be included in the Global Forest Resource Assessment reporting as a separate parameter under "other wooded land", or as "forest area" (if canopy closure exceeds 10 per cent).

All forest in the five countries is mainly state-owned, making it unnecessary to classify ownership. Instead, it would be helpful to provide information on forest tenure, in particular on forest fund land, which is a common tenure category in all five project countries. Forest fund land can be both forested and unforested and is owned, controlled and administered by the forest authorities. Data about the extent of unforested land, which is assigned to the forest fund, or the other land not to be used for agriculture, could give an idea of the potential for afforestation.

Four of the five national C&I for SFM sets also list "protected forest areas" under the criterion on the maintenance and enhancement of the extent of forest resources; even so, a protected forest area is strongly related to the criterion on the maintenance and enhancement of biodiversity. In terms of reporting, this might complicate the assessment and cause misperceptions.

"Growing stock" is a typical indicator that usually accompanies the "area of FOWL", one of the basics for the assessment of forest resources, their condition and use.

The carbon sequestered and stored in forests is an indispensable indicator due to the related UNFCCC reporting obligation, but its measurement is difficult. Most countries base the calculation on the volume of growing stock/biomass, data or estimates for dead wood, litter and below-ground carbon. It is likely that countries will improve the accuracy of their measures of carbon stored in forests by, for example, taking measurements in representative sample plots in each type of forest.

The threshold value for all these assessment parameters would be zero change in the assessment period. The targets should relate to an increase, at least in the low-forest-cover-countries.

4.2 Maintenance of Forest Health and Vitality

Forest health and vitality focuses on adverse stress forests are exposed to, particularly the extent of damage caused by biotic and abiotic factors. Forests in the region face common threats of pests and diseases, forest fires, illegal cutting and overgrazing. Countries have systems in place for the annual recording of damage but there is concern about the reliability of data on overgrazing and illegal cutting.

Key indicators are:

1. Area of FOWL affected by pest and diseases
2. Area of FOWL damaged by forest fires
3. Area of FOWL degraded by illegal logging and volume of wood removed
4. Area of FOWL damaged by overgrazing

The primary consideration within this criterion is to gain a picture of the extent of forest degradation related to the cause. Once a clear picture of the severity of degradation has emerged, further analysis could help to identify specific areas where counteractions could be taken.

National forest inventories can provide general data about damage caused by pests and disease. However, the infrequency and/or irregularity of such surveys limits the usefulness of this source as a basis for countermeasures. Given the scarcity and vulnerability of forest resources in the region, monitoring and assessments on forest health and vitality should be undertaken more frequently (e.g. annually). Ground surveys, supplemented by remote sensing, will identify affected FOWL by the types of damaging agents and the severity of damage.

Data collection on damages, particularly on forest fires, is generally good. Parameters for this indicator are the area damaged, classified by the cause. For fires induced by humans, it is important to distinguish between those caused through ignorance or those deliberately set. Most stakeholders, policymakers and society at large tend to focus more on the area burned, neglecting the causes of fires. This resulted in forestry departments investing mainly in firefighting, rather than fire prevention measures. Focusing on the causes of damage should help decision makers to reshape forest fire prevention strategies.

A common indicator across all five countries is, "area of FOWL degraded by illegal logging and the volume of illegally removed wood". The primary concern is to find out how much ecological and economic damage was caused. Monitoring this indicator is hindered by a lack of accurate data. Much of the illegal cutting was not properly recorded. Even where reliable data was available on the size of devastated areas, there was no information on the volume of illegally logged timber. With the elaboration of new management plans and revised forest codes, more reliable data is expected.

Overgrazing by livestock is widespread in the FOWL in the CCA region. Forestry authorities allow grazing in unforested areas of forest fund land. This permitted grazing is reflected in some C&I for SFM sets under the criterion on the maintenance of the socio-economic functions. Within the forest health and vitality criterion, the aim is to assess the damage caused by uncontrolled grazing, particularly in young forest stands. Remote sensing can help in determining the size of the area damaged by overgrazing. Ground checks can help to confirm findings, identifying if damage is in fact the result of overgrazing or if some other factors are involved.

The threshold value of all the vitality and health related indicators is zero human induced damages; however, realistic targets focus on the reduction of damages.

4.3 Maintenance, Conservation and Enhancement of Forest Biodiversity

Biodiversity is a priority issue for all five countries. Most countries have no adequate monitoring of biodiversity, with the result that there is little data to allow for assessment parameters to be reported. There is a need for expertise and financing, if this situation is to improve. Countries tend to include practical and easy-to-measure indicators to give some picture of the general state of biodiversity in forests, but also need to include those indicators which are relevant to international reporting obligations.

Key indicators are:

1. Protected forest areas
2. Diversity of forest tree stands (by number of tree species per ha)
3. Threatened species (by the International Union for Conservation of Nature (IUCN) classes)
4. Area of FOWL by naturalness (natural, semi-natural and plantations)
5. Regeneration (natural and artificial)
6. Introduced tree species

All five countries have reliable data on the area of protected forests, having inherited a system based on a classification from the Soviet era.

Threatened species are those classified according to IUCN Red Lists. As the Central Asian countries do not have the extensive expert knowledge for assessment, they have no reliable population data for these species and therefore do not include an indicator on threatened species in their sets. In general, countries vary in their capacity to monitor biodiversity, but may at least be able to follow trends with the help of data from systematic observation.

Naturalness is also an important indicator for assessing this criterion. Identifying mono-species plantations should be simple enough. Distinguishing between natural and semi-natural forests represents more of a challenge as the line between them is often blurred.

Naturally regenerated areas are important for safeguarding future habitats for biodiversity. Artificial regeneration may also have a role as harsh conditions and continental climate limit the success of natural regeneration; this means that planting or seeding openings in regenerated areas may be necessary. The focus of this activity is on successfully regenerated areas.

Data on introduced tree species can be extracted from management plans. The share of invasive species should be measured by forestry inventories.

There are no particular thresholds for the assessment parameters of "protected areas" and "threatened species" mentioned in the national sets. However, the common approach for thresholds present in forest management is at least zero change.

The targets for the indicators under the biodiversity criterion relate all to maintenance or enhancement. Improving trends are expected, especially for the area of mixed stands and natural regeneration. The area of natural (undisturbed) forest is expected to be maintained at constant levels.

4.4 Maintenance and Encouragement of Productive Functions of Forests

Productive function covers the amount and sometimes also the value of products and services that forests provide. Quantifying forest ecosystem services is difficult. There were different views on whether to include the monetary value of products and services in this criterion or under the one focusing on socio-economics.

Key indicators are:

1. Roundwood produced
2. Increment and fellings
3. Non-wood products and services

Countries usually have data for wood produced from planned loggings and from sanitary cuts. There are no reliable records of the volume of timber harvested Illegally, which is usually estimated. The volume of illegally harvested wood is significant for some countries and, therefore, should be reported to the extent possible under this or a separate indicator.

The comparison of the amount of harvested wood, against the increment of growing stock in the same period, is an indicator of intensity of forest use. The missing data from the often high shares of illegal cutting will likely distort these calculations. Therefore, assessing removals against increment will need qualitative information on all type of cuts and illegal logging.

Data for the amount and market value of non-wood forest products and services are barely available, as often local people collect many products for subsistence use and there are no systems in place to record such removals. Those data that do exist rely mainly on market values of products or services sold.

The threshold for the parameters "roundwood produced" and "increment", is likely to be no negative change when compared with the ten-year average. The targets focus on an increase of production, provided it does not exceed annual increment.

Potentials are seen to increase the amount and in particular market value of non-wood forest products and services.

4.5 Maintenance and Enhancement of the Protective Functions of Forests

Protective function covers safeguarding soil and water resources, infrastructure and settlements from e.g. erosion, flooding, avalanches. Some of the CCA countries also included indicators on combating desertification and land degradation under this criterion. In such mountainous or arid regions of climatic extremes, this criterion is by far the most significant for monitoring, assessment and reporting of SFM in CCA countries. Quantifying respective parameters was so far difficult. The systematic monitoring of these parameters could significantly support national policy and decision making, help mobilize financial resources and improve the enabling environment for forestry. However, quantifying respective parameters was so far difficult.

There are diverging views regarding the management of protective forests in the CCA region, in particular on the level of human intervention. In many cases, only sanitary cuts are allowed there. However, there also opinions that, like in many other mountainous countries of the world, protective forests should be actively managed to maintain their protective function.

Key indicators are:

1. Forest management for the protection of soil and water
2. Forest rehabilitation/restoration to combat desertification and land degradation

For the first indicator, parameters could include designated protective forests or forests which have conservation as a primary management aim. This second category may include watershed forests, preferably with a defined protective aim in forest management plans. The threshold is zero change of designated protective forest and targets focus on an increased area of forests primarily managed for the protection of soil and water resources.

The second indicator could have parameters monitoring restorations of bare forest land and rehabilitation or afforestation of degraded forest areas; as well as establishment of small-scale woodlots, green belts or other infrastructure and protective facilities against erosion of agricultural soils. There is no threshold for areas rehabilitated to combat desertification

and control erosion but there are ambitions to increase the areas successfully rehabilitated and restored.

4.6 Maintenance of the Socio-Economic Functions of Forests

The socio-economic function demonstrates the importance of forests and forestry in the national socio-economic development of a country. If the respective indicators are well chosen and designed and reported comprehensively, they could attract the interest of policymakers and trigger mobilization of resources to aid the development of the forest sector.

Key indicators are:

1. Value of marketed wood and non-wood products (contribution to GDP)
2. Export and import of timber and wood products
3. Revenue of forest enterprises and forest processing industry
4. Investment in forestry
5. Employment
6. Contribution to rural livelihood
7. Recreation

Most countries have figures for the parameters of the first four economic indicators. Employment in forestry is so far not well documented and government employment records provide only limited data. Forestry departments can supply data for staff and workers on payroll. Data for seasonal workers and part-time employees could come from rural forestry units. Surveys would be needed to capture data for other jobs generated, to provide a complete picture of employment in the forest sector.

Another significant indicator is the contribution that forestry makes to sustaining rural livelihoods. Many poor rural communities depend on forests for their livelihoods. There are no reliable data, unfortunately, for the contribution that wood, non-wood products and services make to help local communities. Parameters for this type of contribution would need to be based on estimates or on special surveys.

The number of recognized sites and forest areas frequented for recreation are parameters for which data are available. Data on the number of visitors need to be based on special surveys.

The targets for nearly all indicators focus on increasing values of these parameters, except for wood imports, where the expectation is to reduce that share due to increasing production and consumption of national wood products.

4.7 Maintenance and Enhancement of the Legal Policy and Institutional Framework

This criterion differs from the first six criteria. It describes the enabling environment, such as the policy, institutional and legal frameworks in relation to forest, forest management and the forest sector. It can help in analysing impact assessment; for example, whether improvements in law enforcement have reduced illegal cutting.

There are two approaches to how to integrate indicators of this group into the C&I sets. They could form a separate criterion, as is proposed in the MP set; or to provide an indicator for other criteria that will describe policies, institutions and instrument related to each criterion, as applied in the Forest Europe concept. The target countries have followed different approaches in constructions of their sets.

Key indicators are:

1. Forest-related legislation (laws, regulations, decrees, international commitments)
2. Forest plans and programmes (national development plans, NFPs, strategy plans)
3. Forest-related institutions (forest-, biodiversity, bioeconomy- or environment-related units, organizations, capacities, resources, effectiveness)
4. Financial and economic instruments
5. Forest education and research

The indicators are mostly descriptive and have no thresholds; the targets generally aim to improve the enabling environment.

5
USE OF CRITERIA AND INDICATORS FOR
SUSTAINABLE FOREST MANAGEMENT
IN OTHER AREAS OF FORESTRY
Assy plateau in Kazakhstan

5. Use of Criteria and Indicators for Sustainable Forest Management in Other Areas of Forestry

5.1 Criteria and Indicators and National Forest Inventory (NFI) – A Tool for Decision Making

Forests satisfy a range of interests and demands, but conflicts can arise when there are competing expectations. NFIs deliver objective, reliable and representative information that provide measures of the ecological, economic and socio-economic benefits of forests.

Tools for informed decision-making in forestry and its importance

Forests are vital for human life, protecting air quality, providing habitats for plants and animals, livelihoods for humans, watershed protection, climate change mitigation and renewable energy and raw materials, including wood.

Forests are resilient, but are affected by changes in land use, forestry operations, climate change or climatic events such as storms, droughts and fires.

Informed decisions on maintaining or enhancing the ability of forests to deliver their multiple benefits need up-to-date, comprehensive, reproducible and reliable information about the state of forests. NFIs are cost-efficient systems for the provision of comprehensive targeted information.

Data assessments and statistics are the core of an NFI

The core elements of NFI are statistical sampling (Figure 3) and mathematics, exact nomenclature and measurements that follow a well-defined protocol.

Statistical sampling is a cost-efficient and reliable method of collecting information, focusing on selected sample locations. Remote sensing using aerial laser scanning, aerial images or satellite images can reduce the need for field work. The strict observance of statistical science principles is essential for gathering accurate and reliable information.

Clear nomenclature requires unambiguous descriptions of terminology, measuring units and measurement rules used for data collection. The starting point of NFI nomenclature is defining forest. The forest definition includes elements of vegetation cover and land use – not all land containing trees is classed as forest – and may be tailored to specific forest structures in a country. Therefore, the definition of forest may differ between countries. FAO has a standard definition for forest, *"Land spanning more than 0.5 hectares with trees higher than 5 metres and a canopy cover of more than 10 per cent, or trees able to reach these thresholds in situ. It does not include land that is predominantly under agricultural or urban land use"*.

Field manuals contain the terminology and exact measuring practices to support accurate and high-quality data collection. Using quality assurance is recommended: this may include a clear definition of staff responsibilities, systematic and documented training, a quality control system for field measurements, including calibration of measuring devices, and data plausibility checks.

NFIs cover the entire forest area of a country but are carried out as sample surveys and not full tallies. The statistical design determines what fraction of the forest area will be sampled. The selected samples are assessed intensively. Expanding the sample data, using statistical methods, provides an assessment of the overall forest extent. As statistical sampling inevitably contains uncertainties, NFI estimates always carry an error. A key element of every sampling procedure is figuring the size of estimation uncertainties by presenting sampling errors for every parameter.

Modelling is an essential part of all NFIs. It is extremely difficult and costly to measure tree volume or biomass directly in the field. Instead, measuring tree diameters and heights allows volume or biomass to be estimated in an efficient way, with the help of statistical models.

Information provided by NFIs

The first stage of setting up an NFI is an information needs assessment. What information is needed? What is the relevant reporting sub-units? How often should information be provided? What level of accuracy is required? NFIs can provide information about:

- Forest area
- Growing stock volume and biomass
- Annual/periodic increment and natural mortality of growing stock
- Annual/periodic fellings
- Biodiversity indicators, such as dead wood and species distribution
- Silvicultural status and forest management
- Forest damage

Information may apply to the entire forest area or sub-units, such as forest type, dominant tree species, ownership or protection status.

NFIs cannot capture information about the status of rare or endangered species, for instance, nor for seasonal features such as mushrooms, or birds/animals that range across large areas of forest. NFIs can only provide habitat data for these

FIGURE 3: **Example of a sampling grid, Germany**

Source: www.bundeswaldinventur.de/weham-2013-bis-2052/das-modell-zum-wald/datengrundlage/
Note: the federal states aggregated the sampling network in different densities

types of information, but no direct observations. The same limitations apply to features of short duration, such as seasonal disturbance by insects or disease.

Merging NFI field and remote-sensing data, such as satellite images, improves the reliability of NFI statistics, especially for sub-national units or small categories. In addition, forest resources can be presented as maps (Figure 4).

NFIs form an important basis for the assessment of sustainability by quantitative indicators and are thus indispensable for the evaluation of the progress towards the sustainability of the multiple function of forest.

Scenario modelling, using NFI data

NFI data provide the basis for a variety of further analyses, using scenario modelling methods. Examples include forecasting future wood supply or the sequestration of atmospheric carbon dioxide by forest growth. Models require assumptions about how different factors might influence forest development. For example, the way climate change or different management approaches affects wood supply or carbon storage. Such scenario analyses make it possible to predict how different approaches to managing forests, such as stopping harvesting, aiming to maximize added value, implementing close-to-nature approaches or increasing forest carbon pools might affect forests in future (Figure 5). Such a tool would describe potential synergies and trade-offs

between the different and sometimes contradictory demands made on forest management.

Institutionalizing NFI

Carrying out an NFI requires:

- Access to all forests, including private land

- A stable budget for a number of years

- Specialists in statistics, mathematical computing, modelling, data management, remote sensing and forest mensuration

- Staff trained in data collection and capable of field work

- Technology and tools for navigation, measurement, data management and information sharing

Forest legislation in many countries already has a provision for regular NFIs. This ensures that objective and representative information on the status and development of forests is available to politicians, the economy, the environment and society.

Involving higher education institutions like universities will help to ensure that up-to-date technical and scientific knowledge is applied.

FIGURE 4: **Forest resource map of Finland based on NFI and satellite images**

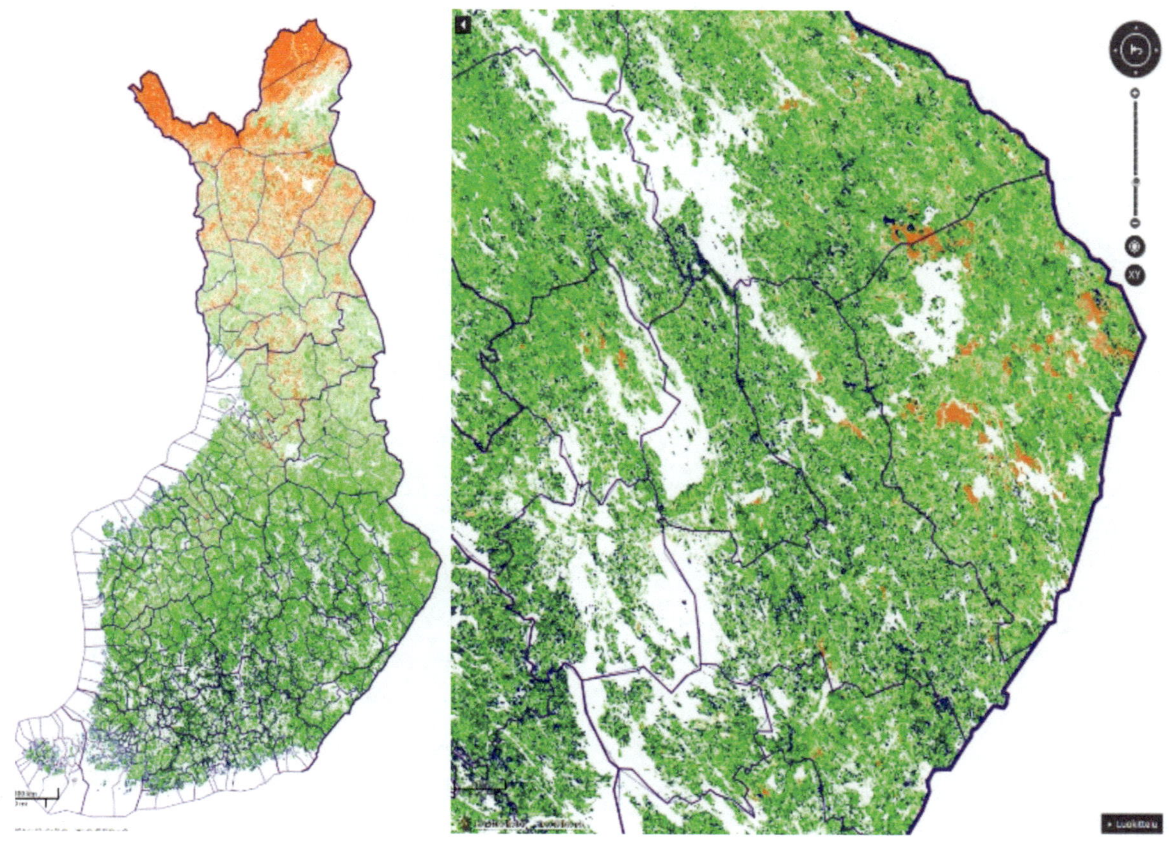

Source: http://www.paikkatietoikkuna.fi/web/en/map-window

FIGURE 5: **Realized development of growing stock volume in Finland in the past and possible future development according to two alternative scenarios**

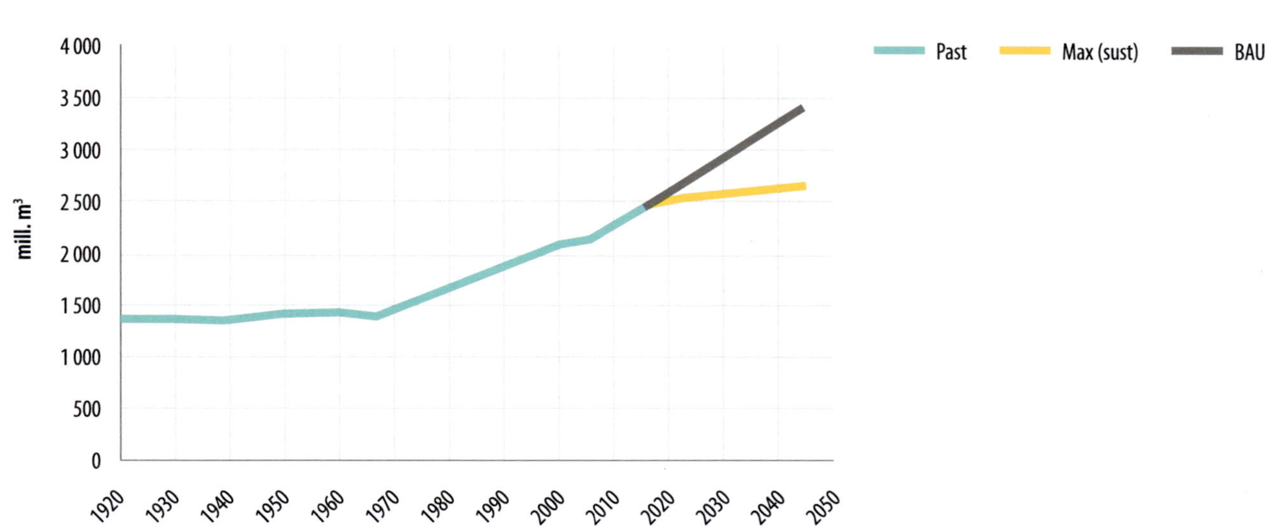

NFI vs. management planning inventories

NFIs serve country-level or regional decision-making policies and monitoring. Management planning inventories cover all forest areas and guide operational forestry decisions at the level of individual forest stands, compartments or forest holdings.

Methods used in management planning inventories cannot produce reliable data for several national level information needs. With current technologies, it is cost-efficient to separate sample based NFIs from management planning inventories. Merging satellite images and NFI field measurements can produce forest resource maps, but the information content is often not sufficient for detailed forest planning.

International aspects

NFIs are also the basis for international reporting on forests. Several international processes are clients of NFIs as they collect forest-related information from various countries. Among these are the Global Forest Resources Assessment, or FRA (FAO), the pan-European reporting of sustainable forest management (UNECE/FAO/Forest Europe), and the UNFCCC. These reporting processes provide guidance on definitions and reporting practice. By presenting information on ecological, economic and social aspects of forest development, they provide a measure, over time, of progress towards SFM at a regional or global level.

The European NFIs have been coordinated through a voluntary ENFIN[32]. This operates as a platform for harmonizing forest inventory information at the European scale. It optimizes synergies between NFIs, shares expertise and supports the adaptation of data collection to current societal and political information needs.

Policy implications

Forest inventories provide information on the multiple benefits supplied by forests. By presenting objective assessments of forest condition, NFIs establish a basis for comparing options for forest management that properly consider synergies and trade-offs.

The way forward

A national forest inventory is an objective and reliable information source about the current state and development of forests. The collection and assessment of information uses scientifically sound methods and web-based tools that allow for public viewing of the information.

It is the main source of information for meeting international forest data reporting obligations, and provides an indispensable tool for all who have responsibility for forests and their sustainable management. Its value in economic and environmental terms far exceeds its cost, but relevant financing must be secured to fully benefit from this tool. It must be undertaken at regular intervals to provide objective information on the current state of forests and assess changes. Therefore, a legal basis should be created for the regular implementation of NFIs.

NFI should cover all types of land-use systems and land-use change, including forest, agriculture, and fallow land, since land use changes over time. It is important as the focus on forest land could result in afforestation being overlooked.

The multi-sectoral nature of NFI renders the involvement of all relevant sectoral institutions, including forestry, agriculture, environment and rural development, necessary. Survey methods and data collected must be adapted to changing information needs for assessing the sustainability of forests in meeting the complex and, at times, competing demands of society.

5.2 Criteria and Indicators and Information Systems – A Tool for Better Forest Policy and Management

Decisions about management of forest resources must be well-informed in order for a forest policy to be effective. In reality, forest policy and management matters are complex and multifactorial, so practical information can be hard to extract.

Information technology advances, and the ease of modern information exchange, have opened opportunities for better management of forest ecosystems and their services. FPMSIS help to gather forest information, making it accessible, informing decisions, monitoring results and modifying current policies. They can increase operational efficiency, reduce cost and supply better information, thereby improving forest ecosystem services and State forest governance. They can also be a strategic tool for economic growth and provide the increased transparency and participation expected by modern society.

The scope of Forest Policy and Management Support Information Systems (FPMSIS)

Forest policy is a complex, multi-disciplinary subject

An effective forest policy needs sound decisions about the maintenance, protection and use of forest resources. Politics itself can be viewed as an exchange of information and opinions connecting all stakeholders in a dynamic system. It requires modelled processes and computer programmes, based on

---

32 ENFIN: http://enfin.info/

current information. Technological tools can help retrieve, process, and provide information to political institutions in an optimal way, leading to effective administration of resources.

Evolving forest policy is a complex process, linked to sustainable development. It is influenced by forest economics, ownership, management planning and law, climate change, bioenergy, afforestation, biodiversity, ecosystem services, land use policy and infrastructure, among others. Forest policy is strongly related to other sectors and, especially nowadays, to public participation and scrutiny on many levels.

FPMSIS aid forest policymaking by gathering forest information to support informed choices, monitoring results, and refining policies.

The main functions of FPMSIS

There are four types of FPMSIS functions used in forest policy and management:

Decision support systems (DSS) – computer programmes intended to assist finding and making informed and efficient decisions, including possible options. They are used at different levels of forest management and policymaking and can include information-visualization tools for policymakers and forest professionals, growth models, systems supporting forest management planning and forest disturbance models.

Distribute functions efficiently

Sometimes, several solution types can be implemented in one system. Poland developed two possible ICT solutions supporting the forest sector:

1. **Information System of State Forests Holding (SFH)** performs the roles of (i) **RMS** for all SFH operations, including workforce management, external services, silvicultural activities, fellings, timber trade and tax calculations and national reporting; (ii) **DSS** for short-term management; (iii) **ISS** for communication within the holding, producing official documents and reports for government agencies and national statistical reporting.

2. **Forest Data Bank** – a national information processing system gathering information on all forests in the country from various sources which serves as: (i) **ISS** – providing source data to various organizations and government agencies, and (ii) **CSS** – running a forest information web portal available to the general public, providing data feeds about forests, compatible with the EU INSPIRE directive to other public and private entities, disseminating NFI results and reports on forest condition and resources in Poland.

Resource management systems (RMS) – utility programmes for resource accounting and distribution. These are commonly used in business, but political institutions also use them to control resources on a continuous basis. Examples include human resources, private investment in public projects, and advanced budgeting and reporting. In forestry, they help the operation of forest administration agencies, forest management enterprises and forest operations enterprises.

Information-sharing systems (ISS) – programmes to arrange the internal structural operations of political institutions and encourage information-exchange within and between public authorities, economic, research and engineering corporations, forest management bodies, private corporations and other organizations. An ISS platform may contain various databases with strategically useful information. Specialized ISS programmes can therefore structure political administration more effectively, moving it from individual to system-based actions. Information sharing about forests can range from a centralized data-sharing hub – a "forest data bank" – through data repositories divided thematically or geographically, to highly distributed systems with strong consistency and interoperability.

Communication support systems (CSS) – specialized software for online use, plus web resources providing interactive political processes to increase social engagement, thereby evolving a 'network society'. CSS are used to publicize strategic information, monitor political information and make the law-development process transparent, thereby adding legitimacy. CSS enable individuals and citizen groups to be involved in different levels of forest-related matters, and to know the latest trends. They create transparent public communication from the forest sector

Components of FPMSIS

Forest policy and management frameworks tend to be country-specific because of country-specific conditions, socioeconomics, political traditions, and other factors. Therefore, forest information systems should be based on the country´s current forestry policy, institutional landscape, organizational capabilities, administrative capacities, and societal needs. At the same time, the forest sector organizational functions are usually similar, even if carried out on different administrative levels. Identifying common elements in those frameworks helps to create effective forest policy and management processes (Figure 6).

The components of the FPMSIS are of various types, as outlined earlier, and perform different organizational functions (Table 1).

TABLE 1: Common elements of FPMSIS and their role in executing various organisational functions of the forest sector

FMPSIS component / Organizational function	Forest Data Bank	Forest Sector Forecasting and Modelling System	Forest Monitoring and Policy Support System	Forest Management Planning Platform	Forest Enterprise Resource Planning System	Support System for Small Forest Owners	Timber Trade Platform	Public Communication Platform
Forest administration / service	Supply of information to decision-making processes.	Timber resources forecasts. Forest damage and fire models. Economic models.	Real-time monitoring of removals and SFM compliance. Information for decision-making.	High-level information for policy decisions about forest management planning.				
Forest management / use				Medium- to low-level information and data for decisions about forest management planning in a forest enterprise.	Operational support and control of all processes of a forest enterprise.	Assistance with decisions about forest property.	Operational support for timber trade processes. Access to timber market for all forest owners.	
Forest operation performing					Operational support and control (if not done by contractor).	Operational support and control. / Knowledge base & information exchange with other owners.		
Forest operation supervision / control					Operational support and control of supervision processes over forest operation contractors.			
Forest supervision (including timber supply chain supervision)	Data gathering and integration about fellings, timber trade, forest condition, and calamities.		Providing up-to-date information for supervision of forest condition and forest-related processes.			Data and tools for proper supervision of forest estate.	Operational support for timber supply chain supervision.	
Timber consumption and trade	Gather and share data about economic aspects of forest utilization, including timber trade and consumption.					Easy access to timber market for small forest owners.	Providing easy and equal access to timber market.	
Social dialog / participatory processes	Provide all necessary background information for participatory processes on various forest-related topics.			Provide transparent information about forest planning process and facilitate feedback and discussion. / Facilitate information exchange between stakeholders of forest management planning process.				Provide the public with the means to interact with nfrmto political and sharig administrative bodies in forest and forestry matters.
Public communication	Share extensive, detailed, accurate and transparent public data about forests. / Provide extensive, detailed, accurate and transparent public data about forests for other purposes.							Provide transparent and accurate information for the public about forest ecosystems, including real-time information (fire danger, entry bans), forest sector policies and legislation.

Legend: Decision support ■ Resource management ■ Information sharing ■ Communication support

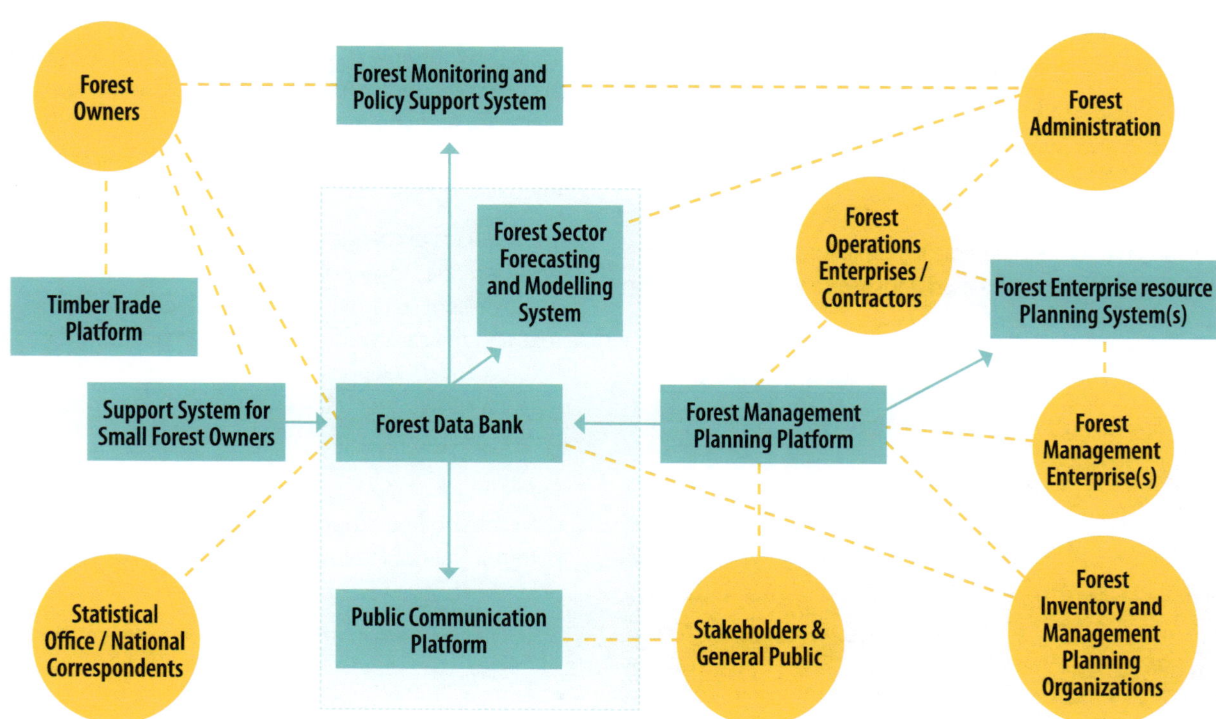

The relevance of these components depends on individual country conditions. For example, if the forest sector has limited capacity owing to physiographical or historical reasons, there is no need to implement all the Figure 6 components. Some functions can be simplified and combined in multipurpose units.

Some components are commonly used because they support "traditional" functions of the forest sector, such as systems which help run forest management operations. Others have appeared only recently – for example, communication platforms, and monitoring and modelling systems. These have become relevant with the development of information technologies, climate change awareness, certification requirements and changing societal attitudes. Some modules can also be country-specific, addressing management structures. Every module requires information, which sometimes cannot be secured, for political, economic or organizational reasons.

Benefits of having FPMSIS

Information systems can improve operational efficiency, reduce costs, provide decision-makers with better, more complete, information, and thereby improve forest ecosystem services and state governance. They also bring additional benefits, such as reducing information processing errors, increasing its efficiency and facilitating integration of information.

They can provide:

- Custom data for a specific task or decision-making process.
- Custom formats which can be tailored to the needs of their users, for example lists and charts.
- Real-time data - particularly useful when rapid action is needed, like dealing with illegal logging or calamities.
- Data about the past, particularly useful for reports, analysis and business planning.

From a temporal perspective, FPMSIS gives users the following advantages:

1. Better understanding of the current situation. ICT knowledge-management systems store data about the current state of a topic and provide tools to help acquire it. Examples of this include forest inventories and monitoring. They can also offer statistical analysis of this data.

2. Predicting changes. ICT tools can use existing information to provide predictive statistics, expert-based heuristics and various modelling approaches.

3. Formulating solutions. ICT tools help to manage knowledge about the root causes of scenarios and situations. They can analyse data and help decision-

making on various levels: landscape, forest, project/management unit and forest management planning.

4. Implementing solutions. There is evidence that properly used ICT tools increase operational efficiency, for example by automating standard operations. They also improve process quality, promote synergy of actions and help manage information flow. Therefore, they can optimize costs and improve results.

FPMSIS can also be a strategic resource for economic growth and a solution for the increased transparency and participation modern societies expect.

How to develop a national FPMSIS infrastructure

Think of alternatives

Recently developed ideas in adaptive management show it may not be feasible or cost-effective to have complete solutions for problems in a complex multi-dimensional system like the forest sector. It is better to spend less on finding optimal solutions and more on monitoring to detect and correct failures as early as possible. This approach may need new FMPSIS elements to provide data about new needs, and to limit the scope of other elements with high costs and limited benefits.

Choose the right approach and size

Begin by designing the information systems around the forest management strategy, following from existing forest policy, the institutional landscape, organizational and financial capabilities and administrative capacity.

The first step is to analyse how the forest sector is organized and determine need and opportunity for improvements, especially those which would have the greatest effect. A cost-effectiveness analysis should ensure the correct project scope has been chosen.

The most important stakeholders should be involved early in this analysis, especially key process participants. They understand their business better than external consultants and have practical experience to evaluate needs, opportunities and potential drawbacks. The analytical process should be coordinated by a moderator equally distant to all stakeholders, proving neutrality, balance and fairness.

Achieving a consistent, effective system within forest sector financial and organizational constraints can be a problem. Processes must be analysed to determine which should be changed and which replaced. It is advisable to determine funds available for building and maintaining FPMSIS components.

Sometimes, a country may have some FPMSIS components already functioning. These should be analysed to determine how well they fit current expectations. If they fit well, they should be improved rather than replaced, as users will be accustomed to them. However, sometimes for technical efficiency and compatibility with other components, the old system must be completely rebuilt while keeping its user interface and process structure.

The total cost of changes should be evaluated against potential gains. An often-overlooked aspect is hidden cost of business processes not suiting how people and organizations see their role, and the ease with which they can operate processes.

The role national SFM C&I can play in forest management and policy

Forest management and policy are complex domains, so they must be conceptually streamlined for efficiency and communication. Useful tools in this context, include C&I for SFM. These have several functions:

1. Outlining a country's area of competence or interest in SFM.

2. Providing a tool to measure SFM progress.

3. Providing a structure for forest inventory and national forest reporting.

4. Optimizing the number of parameters measured.

5. Facilitating the process which communicates information to the user.

C&I for SFM can therefore be meaningful representations of real conditions in forest ecosystems and the forest sector.

The country's criteria and indicator framework are a point of reference for forest policy monitoring and communication and should be connected to a general model of the forest sector. This should integrate political strategies and forces present in the sector, as well as plans for management action and feedback on outcomes. Supporting tools can be arranged around it.

A good example of this approach is the driving force–pressure–state–impact–response (DPSIR) framework used by the European Environment Agency for reporting activities (see Figure 7). With this framework, social and economic developments exert pressure on the environment, causing changes in environmental parameters. These can have impacts on human health, ecosystems, materials, and ecosystem services, which may lead to social responses. Indicators are an easy-to-grasp way of describing and monitoring these processes.

Having a C&I system for SFM linked to knowledge-management systems as well as modelling and planning platforms enables managers and policymakers to make informed decisions

FIGURE 7: **A driving force–pressure–state–impact–response (DPSIR) framework example**

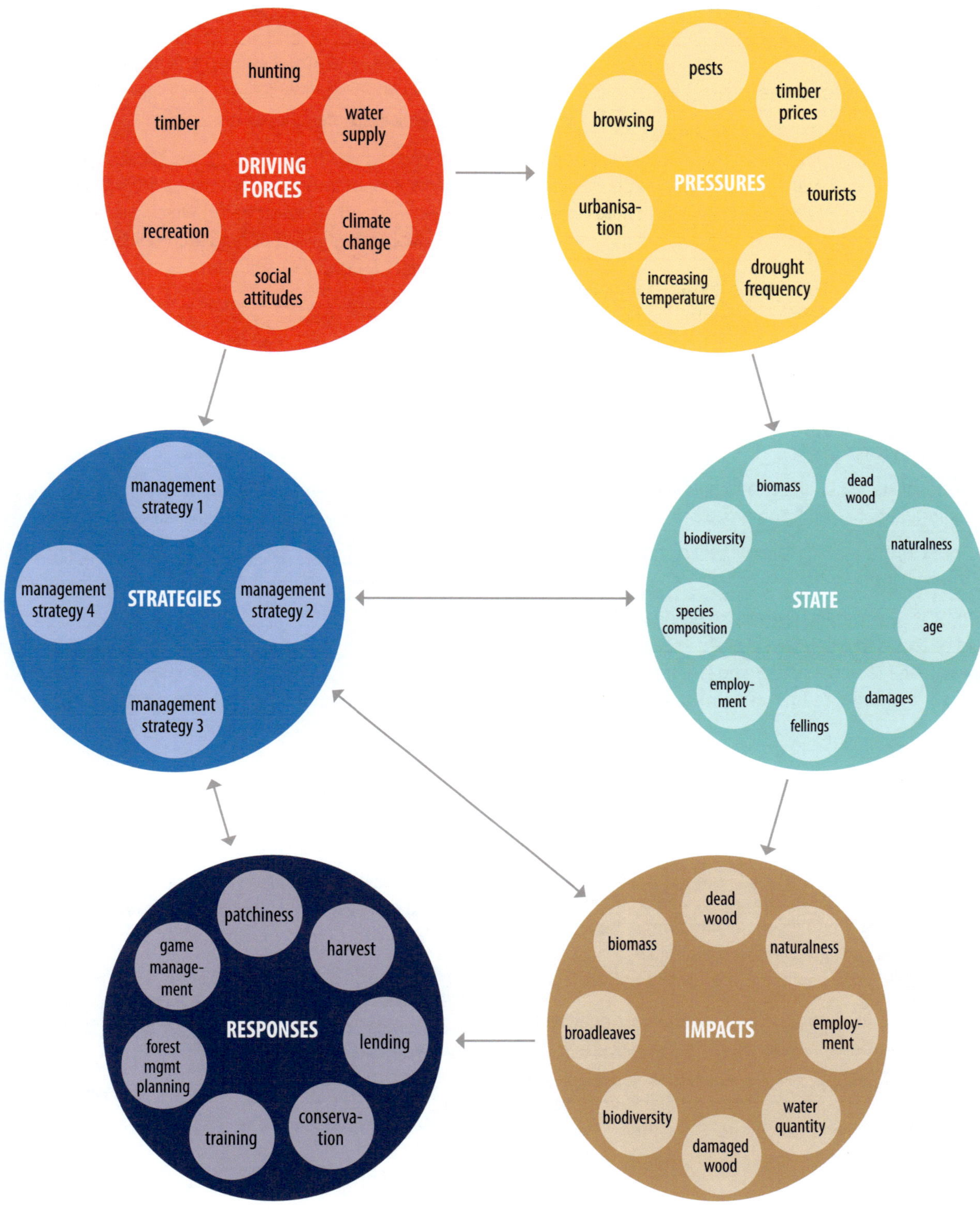

based on a comprehensive, easy-to-grasp view of the current situation and its dynamics. It should be a central element, defining the scope and structure of the information system and linking major stakeholders, including professions such as surveyors and the general public.

The main actors that need to be involved

The main actors needed will vary depending on how forest administration is organized in a country, as well as factors such as forest ownership structure, natural conditions, level of economic development and social attitudes towards forestry.

The actors should include:

- Public administration – ministries, agencies responsible for forests and forestry (usually environmental or agricultural sector).
- Other governmental agencies.
- Forest management organizations.
- Forest owners.
- National statistical offices and national correspondents for international reporting processes.
- Forest inventory and management planning groups, and research institutions.

For FPMSIS development, specialists outside the forest sector should be included wherever possible. These should include business management experts and ICT strategic designers. They can provide options and insights from different perspectives.

Gradual progress usually works better

Even after careful analysis and identification of intervention areas and expected results, FPMSIS elements should not be all implemented simultaneously. Implementation of new ICT tools must fit organizational and procedural changes. This is usually difficult, as it requires modifying human behaviour. It is advisable to use an iterative development approach, which brings the additional benefit of distributing cost over time.

It is best to identify FPMSIS components most needed by stakeholders – these will be more readily accepted. For instance, if the highest-scoring impediment is accessing information, start by building a forest databank which serves many stakeholders and processes. Or, if there is a major concern about illegal logging, a timber-tracking system should be implemented first.

After successful deployment, those involved in the project will acquire experience, practical knowledge of difficulties and technical and organizational expertise. These can be shared and used in the next stages. There will also be satisfied stakeholders spreading the news about the successful solution, making it easier to convince others in future.

However, all of this should be within a well-defined FPMSIS creation or extension programme. A coordinator with powerful prerogatives should be appointed; the coordinator's task will be to ensure cohesion and interoperability between systems, processes and operating procedures, especially among different organizations. They can be based at the ministry responsible for forestry, the national forestry agency or a dedicated inter-agency task force.

This coordinator must have strong support from decision makers. People and institutions naturally tend to defend areas of influence and will resist change which directly affects them. An FPMSIS design without proper coordination and support may lead to suboptimal solutions.

An example process for building FPMISIS

1. Make the political decision to build an FPMSIS.
2. Appoint a coordinator responsible for the whole programme.
3. Identify and invite stakeholders.
4. Analyse the current situation, needs, requirements and opportunities, with the participation of all stakeholders.
5. Perform a cost-benefit analysis of options, considering resources available to develop and maintain FPMSIS components.
6. Create a master plan, defining a minimum viable solution and options. This should identify desired FPMSIS components, their purposes, their positions in the organizational structure, expected outcomes and responsibility for operation and maintenance.
7. Build a roadmap, choosing what to implement first considering most urgent needs, available resources and organizational capacity.
8. Carry out a single FPMSIS component project. This must be supervised by the coordinator to ensure compatibility with other FPMSIS components and avoid functional duplication.
9. Make necessary legislative and organizational changes. Provide prerogatives and ensure funding for component maintenance.
10. Evaluate results and modify master plan as appropriate.
11. Repeat steps 8-10 as necessary.

Need for sustainability of the system

FPMSIS development is a cutting-edge innovation, significantly advancing forest information management and bringing many benefits to policymakers, stakeholders and society in general. However, to guarantee full functionality, users must construct the right technology and undergo organizational change. Success depends on those involved fully understanding both benefits and related requirements and accommodating them in action. Implementation of technical solutions cannot be separated from changes in, for example, procedures, guidelines and reporting formats. Sometimes, even legislative adjustments may be required. There is a need to invest in key-user training to create awareness of the system's capabilities and enable efficient use.

Successful FPMSIS implementation also needs continuous availability, updating, and adapting to meet changing conditions and stakeholder demands. Building the system requires installation of permanent information-updating processes, maintenance procedures and periodic assessments of a good fit to current needs.

There must also be stable funding mechanisms to keep the system running and provide the returns on the investment in FPMSIS.

Policy implications

Building a successful forest policy and management support information infrastructure must be driven by a high-level political decision.

A strategic plan is needed, with a coordinator or coordinating body with adequate prerogatives.

All key forest sector stakeholders and actors must be engaged, assisted by technical experts.

A thorough analysis of the forest sector's current structure, tools, requirements and needs is necessary to identify the most effective interventions and to decide if key elements will be created or if existing elements can be improved.

The scope of the FMPSIS must fit a country's forest-sector financial and organizational constraints. Funding must be secured for creating and maintaining FPMSIS components.

The way forward

Good policymaking and management require tools for acquiring and reporting information, monitoring outcomes and making necessary adjustments. Information systems are an indispensable part of modern governance.

Forest sector information systems should be aligned to forest management strategy, institutional landscape, organizational and financial capabilities and overall administration capacities.

5.3 Criteria and Indicators-based International Monitoring, Assessment and Reporting

Monitoring, assessment and reporting (MAR) on forests have been part of global and national forest policy and management systems for many decades.

A C&I-based MAR system supports quantitative implementation of the three pillars of sustainable development. Governments and international organizations acknowledge the role of C&I in SFM implementation. Many international agencies, including those that are part of the UN, promote MAR and support countries' implementation of it.

Monitoring, Assessment and Reporting in global forest policy and management

After the Rio Summit, international forest negotiations continued for the following decade, resulting in more than 270 proposals for action to translate international goals into country actions (see Figure 8). In 2000, the UNFF was established to implement these actions. This international arrangement for forests would "monitor and assess progress at the national, regional and global levels through reporting by Governments, as well as by regional and international organizations, institutions and instruments, and on this basis consider future actions needed".

The UNFF and the Collaborative Partnership on Forests endorsed the development of a MAR system to show how participating countries implemented these actions. The UNFF promoted use of C&I to frame global forest reporting to assess country progress towards SFM (FAO 2003).

Meanwhile, other international bodies, some forest-specific, recognized the use of indicators as information tools for decision-making and monitoring. A range of indicator-based reporting was initiated by the United Nations Commission on Sustainable Development, UNCBD, UNCCD and non-United Nations bodies such as the Organisation for Economic Co-operation and Development and the Center for International Forestry Research.

UNFF adopted in 2007, a non-legally binding Instrument on Management, Conservation and Sustainable Development of All Types of Forests, hereafter called the Forest Instrument. Member States committed themselves to implement a series of policies and measures that are necessary to achieve sustainable forest management. They agreed to monitor and assess progress towards achieving the objectives of the Forest Instrument, and to submit, voluntarily, national progress reports as part of their regular reporting to the UNFF.

Although substantial efforts have been made in institutional development, governance and policy progress worldwide

FIGURE 8: Milestones of forest-related issues in the global international agenda 1992-2021

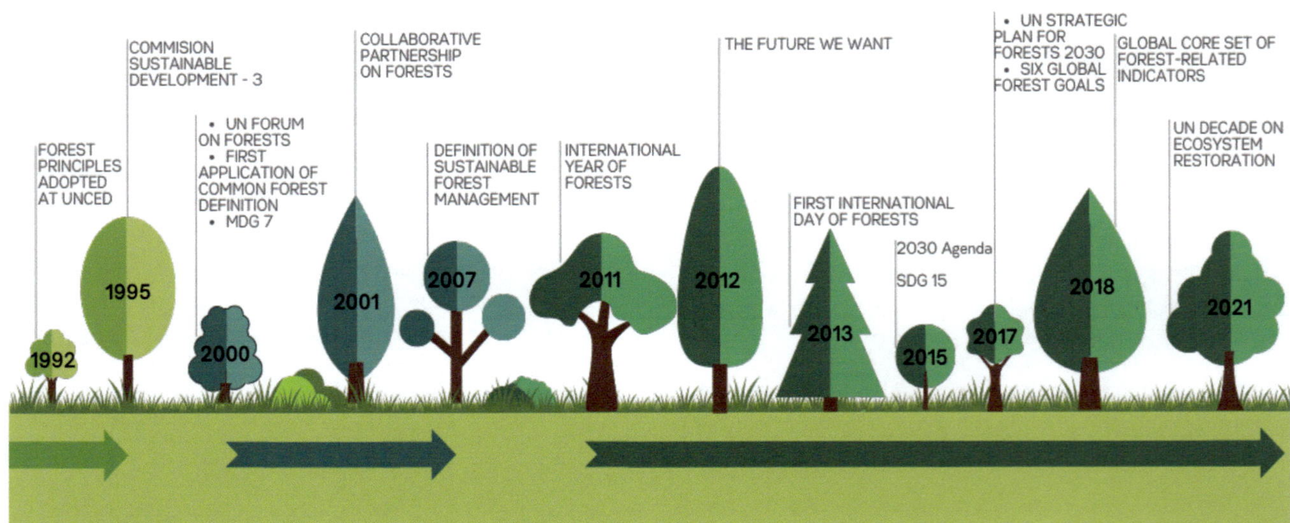

(Sotirov *et al.*, 2020), until now governments negotiating within the UNFF have found no legally binding consensus. Meanwhile many African and European countries are moving away from the policy idea of a non-legally binding Instrument (Rayner at al., 2010). However, global forest governance is vital to reducing forest loss due to climate change.

Governments adopted the UN Strategic Plan for Forests 2017-2030, and 26 associated targets that took a holistic approach, treating forests as necessary for human survival and the environment (Sommer, 2020). This policy development renewed the focus on C&I and on MAR (Arnold *et al.*, 2014).

The adoption of the United Nations Sustainable Development Agenda, its SDGs and the Paris Agreement of the UNFCCC created another turning point, by increasing country participation in implementation (Dzebo *et al.*, 2019). This created opportunities for large-scale transformational collective solutions, where forests play a vital role in achieving the SDGs.

The need for Monitoring, Assessment and Reporting

MAR on SFM has been a key area of work for the UNFF since its establishment. MAR is a basis for decision-making on forest policy and management and allows the measurement of progress towards the implementation of UNFF actions. MAR aids countries and national organizations in making policy decisions, based on national data, and, at a broader scale, international level organizations, such as the FAO. The FRA, UNFF and UNCBD compile national data to provide reports for different users. From the outset, UNFF stressed the need for monitoring systems that allowed data sharing and would streamline global forest reporting.

MAR needs to be straightforward and to support systematic collection and analysis of forest data that will generate national statistics. Sound data and information are fundamental for a country's forest protection, restoration and sustainable management, as well as for United Nations agreements and conventions that relate to forests, including the SDGs, such as SDG 15.

MAR aligns national forest policies with up-to-date, reliable, transparent and accessible information. Thereby, the opportunity for harmonizing MAR with national forest programmes, as well as the Forest Law Enforcement, the Governance and Trade Action Plan, and REDD+ initiatives is offered.

As part of the policy cycle, MAR supports strategic planning and policymaking by showing the links between policy interventions, outcomes, and impacts. This legitimizes the allocation and use of public resources and enhances policy effectiveness. A good MAR framework enables countries to respond to multi-purpose national needs for forest information. Assessing and reporting SFM progress requires monitoring at differing levels, with periodic aggregation at larger scales to show where corrective action may be needed. MAR helps forest and land managers to improve management plans and to see the effects of forest management practices. Lastly, MAR informs the public about forest health and sustainable forest management.

What are the differences between Monitoring, Assessment and Reporting?

MAR covers the three key tasks of UNFF to implement the proposals for action that advances SFM: monitoring, assessment and reporting. The three components of MAR are synergistic and tightly connected.

Monitoring, means periodic quantitative measurements of a specific parameter or qualitative collection of additional relevant information. Monitoring by itself, is not enough to assess progress towards SFM.

Assessment is the analysis and synthesis of information that allows interpretation of the data for every indicator to express progress towards SFM. Assessment specifies the information that needs to be gathered, focusing on situations and trends - for example, how SFM activity can change forest condition, such as increased growing stock or protected biodiversity. Assessment can provide a more balanced and integrated interpretation of the performance of different forest components.

Reporting is necessary to pass on assessment results for policy, planning and management actions to achieve progress towards SFM (FAO, 2011). This is vital for the follow-up of forest management activities to inform about interventions to optimize SFM impact. It is also important that MAR for SFM should use easily comprehensible reports and be action-oriented at the international, national and regional level.

MAR links these three components into a coherent and efficient system for data collection, for the development of indicators, assessments and information to support decision-making and progress towards SFM.

Actors involved in Monitoring, Assessment and Reporting

Successful MAR examples demonstrate the importance of broad stakeholder participation, consensus and acceptance to achieving sustainable forest management.

For over 25 years, national and international actors have been involved in developing C&I for SFM (Linser *et al.*, 2018a). MAR draws upon many sources of data and information, including remote sensing, field observation, maps, reports, other documents and expert information. Data on diverse forest attributes are recorded, stored and processed, serving indicators to obtain policy-relevant information.

Involving forest research, education and training institutions ensures that MAR is updated using the latest technology and approaches.

The similarity among these countries and organizations is striking and occurs since they all use MAR structured around a set of C&I for SFM that cover a broad range of forest benefits.

The processes differ in structure and content, such as the number of national-level criteria, and level of assessment considered. Participating countries commented on the lack of coordination among the various C&I for SFM processes, as well as a lack of harmonized definitions. This has contributed to unclear messages, and an unnecessarily high reporting burden.

What are the steps to develop a MAR in a country?

There is no single best way for developing MAR on SFM. However, in 2009, 12 countries in the Asia Pacific region developed globally harmonized forest-related national MAR which is a useful example[33]. The guidelines and the structure of the database for MAR on SFM could be applied in any other region.

The initial phases of MAR set-up include development and implementation. The development phase focuses on international activities. Examples include linkages with forest-related processes and development of a globally harmonized framework, or the development of technical guidelines, basic database structure and information-sharing networks for MAR. All these ensure that MAR are linked and harmonized with processes, protocols and reports at the international level. This will help to develop national forest policies and plans, using the information supplied by MAR. This phase usually involves close collaboration with FAO.

The implementation phase is conducted at the country level. It includes implementing a framework and guidelines, as well as database structure and information networks. An essential early step is to set up a network of national focal points for national, regional and international monitoring and data collection. This ensures the national MAR system is efficient and will contribute to SFM. It also involves awareness-raising among major stakeholder groups, sectors and actors.

Further MAR development may differ broadly between countries. Issues and measures can be identified and discussed at sub-regional and national workshops to:

- Harmonize definitions.

- Identify approaches for data compilation and review.

- Build capacity by providing primary methodologies for forest policy review and linking it with the national planning processes.

- Establish a national and regional database of internationally harmonized elements or variables that facilitate description of the status and assessment of trends in national forest management and policies.

---

33 http://www.fao.org/forestry/mar/34909@86134/en/

- Develop an information-sharing network of regional and national focal points of forest-related agencies and processes, project focal points and relevant stakeholders.

Other models could be used to develop similar frameworks and guidelines, for example the triangular model of ecological, economic and social dimensions of sustainability and the Driver-Pressure-State-Impact-Response (DPSIR) model. Any approach must be flexible, and match country capacity for forest information and management systems. A country's MAR essential elements must also maintain international compatibility with regional and international MAR frameworks.

Monitoring and reporting remain a challenge for countries that lack human and financial capacity or adequate means/methods to carry out a forest inventory. Many countries need to develop standard methods to gather information about non-timber forest benefits, socio-economic indicators and coherent data on financing SFM. Many countries also need guidelines on collecting timely, comparable and consistent forest information (see COFO, 2012).

The FAO has supported member countries with national forest monitoring for over 70 years. Their Voluntary Guidelines for National Forest Monitoring show how countries can build multipurpose MAR for SFM, supporting national decision-making and international reporting. The UNECE carried out regional studies and developed guidelines to support C&I for SFM (UNECE 2019 a and b).

Regular updating of MAR generates innovation by identifying new ways to fast-track technical capacity development and improve technology transfer. Systems for earth observation, data access, processing, forest monitoring analysis and open-source software enable accurate, efficient and cost-effective forest MAR.

Policy implications

The set-up of a national MAR system facilitates the use of C&I to monitor and assess national trends in forest conditions and management in a number of ways.

Further promotion of C&I and MAR relies on increasing political commitment.

Continuous technical support and guidance should be offered to countries to apply C&I effectively and to encourage non-participating countries to use them.

The same is true for strengthening concepts and definitions and for supporting the C&I processes.

The development of C&I should innovatively optimize resource management and simplify application.

The way forward

MAR naturally occur in local, national and international systems, demanded by legislative, managerial rules or participation in international arrangements. However, the way they are carried out and organized varies greatly among countries. An organized monitoring, assessing and reporting system for SFM may substantially increase efficiency and effectiveness of related work, as well as consistency and credibility of processed information. Components of such a system include:

1. Clearly expressed goals, and a set of C&I to measure and track progress and performance.

2. A set of guidelines for all responsible actors and implied stakeholders to inform and report to each other.

3. An opportunity for responsible actors to meet periodically to coordinate action and review progress.

The joint UNECE/FAO Forestry and Timber Section[34] supports developing evidence-based policies for SFM and communicates about the many products and ecosystem services provided to society, while assisting countries of the region to monitor and manage forests.

Through a United Nations Development Account (UNDA) project, the UNECE/FAO have given technical assistance to countries in Eastern and South-Eastern Europe, the Caucasus and Central Asia. This capacity-building supports SFM, data collection, monitoring and analysis and the engagement of national experts in these regions. The outcomes of regional workshops and reports are available on the UNECE/FAO/UNDA project website[35].

5.4 Criteria and Indicators for Forest-related Communication

The purpose of communicating about forests

There is growing interest in forestry matters at every stage of the forester's work, starting with operational practice, through local and national planning and development, to international policy initiatives. Everyone, whether citizen, nature lover, businessperson, tourist, government official or politician, wants to know what is happening in local, regional, national and global forests.

Public communication serves many purposes. The overriding purpose is to provide information to aid better understanding.

For some of the society, forests are nice to look at; to visit for recreation, a run in the morning or walking a dog. Others recognize the environmental and economic value of forests, in addition to their social and cultural benefits. Forests provide

---

34 Joint UNECE/FAO Forestry and Timber Section: http://www.unece.org/forests/welcome.html

35 UNECE/FAO/UNDA project: https://unece.org/forests/accountability-systems-sustainable-forest-management-caucasus-and-central-asia

employment, timber for everyday products and support livelihoods, often in fragile rural communities.

As understanding of the myriad benefits offered by forests increases, the challenge for communicators intensifies, requiring reliable, scientifically sound information and powerful tools to present the evidence that demonstrates assigned values. C&I for SFM are such a tool.

C&I help by showing the complexity of forests and forestry and by considering the range of uses and potential values that society assigns to forest resources.

Adler and Towne (1978) state that every human accomplishment will involve communication with others[36]. This is ever more relevant today, with references to forests in almost all major international commitments and reporting obligations, including SDG reporting[37], FRA and UNFCCC[38].

The target audience for communication about forests and forestry

As with any area, communication about forests and forestry may target individuals, involve dialogue between specific groups or be directed at the general public. Communication may be undertaken by international organizations; State institutions, including ministries and government agencies; forest administration at every level; specialized communication units, stakeholder organizations and even individual foresters.

Successful communication will cover all three dimensions of sustainable forest management: economic, environmental and social aspects. It relies on identification of target audiences. These audiences may be individuals, groups and communities that have influence and decision-making power over the forest sector. Forestry is under scrutiny, with often strongly held, and sometimes contradictory opinions, emerging in public discussions. When transmitting information about forest matters, it is necessary to consider those who might react positively to the messages and also to respect those whose views may differ. Additionally, not all target audiences will have the same level of understanding of issues; some audiences may be new to the topic, or from outside the forestry/environmental sector and its overall business. For communication with these audiences to be effective, there must be a careful assessment of their current understanding, the factors driving their interest and their connections with the forestry sector. Remember too that target audiences may have

links with the people who have influence over decisions: this may include family members, friends, leaders and the media.

Questions that help to identify target audiences

- What message or information do you want to communicate?
- Whose attitudes and behaviours are you trying to affect?
- Who are the influencers?
- Who must be moved to action?
- Who has the greatest impact on the outcome?
- Who will affect whether you fail or succeed?

Questions that help to clarify the involvement of target audiences

- Does the target audience need to be more aware of something?
- Does the target audience need to change its attitude?
- Does the target audience need to change its behaviour?
- Should our communications be more informative or engaging?
- What kinds of reputational risks are there?

In analysing potential target groups[39], it is important to understand how they perceive problems and what sparked their interest in forestry. Some people may be interested in emerging issues like climate change, others in protecting biodiversity and still others in timber production. Just as the concept of SFM integrates different aspects of forestry, forest-related communication needs to recognize the different standpoints and interests within society and stakeholder groups. It is worth trying to engage with those people or organizations that may be able to influence change, and in that way to multiply and extend the reach of "our" message.

Developing a communication strategy

There is no single approach to developing a successful communication strategy. Certain steps can ensure that the design of a strategy helps the forest organization to communicate effectively and to meet its objectives. It is not surprising that forestry issues are seen and understood differently by those in the forestry community and the public.

---

36 Basic communication model: https://docplayer.net/1652142-Basic-communication-model.html

37 Basic communication model: https://docplayer.net/1652142-Basic-communication-model.html

38 Land use, land-use change and forestry under the Convention: https://unfccc.int/land-use-land-use-change-and-forestry-under-the-convention

39 How to determine your target audience https://publicrelationssydney.com.au/how-to-determine-your-target-audience/

TABLE 2:   **Target groups for forest-related communication**

Who are they?	Why are they important?
• Policymakers: national, regional and local politicians, ministers and policy leaders. • Relevant civil organizations: NGOs from various sectors relevant to forestry. • Institutional and market decision makers within related sectors and industries: environmental (climate change) and renewable energy sectors, agriculture; construction. • Key media people: journalists/other media commentators at national, regional or local level. • Education system – administrators, teachers and children. • General public.	• Participate in many legislative processes, including consultations and lobby activities; some of them view their role as a watchdog organization for critically monitoring the activities of governments, industry. • Play a central role when it comes to creating forest policy, legislative regulations, governance and supervision of forest sector development. • Influence cross-sectoral decisions that may results in long-term direction for developments and trades-off between different sectors. • Shape people's views, serving as channels for transmitting information and influence the image of an organization. • Partners in forest education. • Very important for gathering support for the forest sector activities and maintaining a social license to

Developing a communication strategy[40] should begin with identifying the present state of public perception of forests and forestry, the main areas of interest and any gaps, including misperceptions of forest management. These efforts are even more important when considering the broader context of how forests and their potential have emerged on the global political agenda in line with the Sustainable Development Goals and the Paris Agreement, for example. These open opportunities for communication, information and actions to rebalance knowledge gaps and to provide a deeper understanding of forests and forestry.

Useful tools for developing a communication strategy[41] when analysing the current situation are:

a)   SWOT Analysis - identifying the forest sector's **Strengths, Weaknesses, Opportunities, and Threats**.

b)   PEST Analysis - identifying the **Political, Economic, Social and Technological factors** that could affect the forest sector or a forest organization's work.

Whatever approach is used, a communication strategy will need to include information about target audience, goals and tailored messages, as well as a team of inspired people to implement the plan.

Who should be involved in communicating forest-related issues?

Whether it consists of forestry people in media units or an outside organization, such as a public relations agency, an effective communication team must be professional and have the required competencies. The strategy should supply everyone within the forestry organization with the information and messages to communicate, maintain a consistent approach to planned activities and avoid ambiguity. Communication responsibilities may follow a range of models. A standard model is assigning most communication tasks to a nominated spokesperson or a specialized media unit. Many forestry organizations have operational units with personnel who specialize in communicating and explaining specific issues. In some, there are staff specialized in forest education or leading tours and lessons about forests.

Tools to communicate forestry issues

There are many communication tools and methods available and choosing one will depend on the budget and what is known to work best for the chosen audience. Social media are used more and more, but traditional methods, such as

---

40   Guidelines and tools for developing communication strategies for joint UN teams on AIDS https://www.unaids.org/sites/default/files/media_asset/jc1582_guidelines_tools_en_3.pdf

41   Developing a communication strategy https://knowhow.ncvo.org.uk/campaigns/communications/communications-strategy

Best practice example from Poland

The State Forests in Poland established a separate department for national outreach, known as the State Forests Information Centre, about 20 years ago. It publishes magazines and books, runs the State Forests website, operates social media profiles and organizes promotional information and events. It has run many successful campaigns including, *"Welcome – the forests: a good neighborhood"* in 2017. The aim of the campaign was to show that forests looked after by State Forests met the highest standards of management, taking full account of the social, ecological and economic expectations of society. Coordinated activity increases the strength and impact of communication messages. The Centre publishes and distributes periodicals on forest and forestry: an internal monthly magazine and a quarterly magazine aimed at people who are interested in forests, mainly tourists and forest enthusiasts, teachers and pupils. Social media is now the most popular tool for communication, with half a million followers; the official profile of the State Forests at Instagram receives considerable attention, as well as the Twitter profile. Another popular move was the establishment of a forest educational portal, Las Rysia eRysia (**https://www.lasy.gov.pl/pl/edukacja**), which explains biodiversity of forests and how they influence the environment and climate. This forest education platform is dedicated to the public at large, but the main target is the young generation. The platform includes three sites: for primary schoolchildren (grades 4-6), for intermediate schoolchildren and for teachers. The portal receives an average of 20,000 visits monthly, with the thematic blogs *"Forester's blog"* and *"Forest Educator's Blog"*. It offers a foundation for raising awareness among the young generation about our shared responsibility for the condition of the environment.

press briefings, factsheets, calendars, advertising, indoor and outdoor exhibitions, posters, podcasts or photography should not be overlooked. Consider engaging directly with members of Parliament and research communities as a way of advocating on specific topics with legislators.

Outreach on forestry topics

Outreach activities create a link between the forest sector and stakeholder groups, helping to promote SFM. Special events, including outdoor activities, enhance public appreciation of the importance of forests and their role in supplying multiple economic, social and environmental benefits. Outreach can include press and news releases, thematic media campaigns and organizing events, such as outdoor education for school groups. Websites and social media are of increasing importance and have become a significant means of communication. The challenge is to keep websites, Facebook pages and Twitter looking fresh, up-to-date and attractive.

There are international opportunities to boost forest communication across the wider community inside and outside the forest sector; it is recommended to take advantage of these. The United Nations International Day of Forests, held annually on 21 March, promotes the importance of forests and trees for people and the planet.

The United Nations cooperate with governments, community organizations, forest administrations and the public to promote local and global activities dedicated each year to a chosen theme. The International Day highlights specific topics each year of forests and seeks synergies with other sectors. When the forestry community acts collectively, it strengthens the power of the message at different levels, giving it greater attention, visibility and impact.

Networking and collaboration are essential. The UNECE/FAO Forest Communicators' Network[42] provides a forum for international interaction and cooperation in forest-related communication[43]. The FCN has undertaken many activities, which have improved the ability of the forest sector to communicate within and outside the sector.

---

42   UNECE-FAO Forest Communicators Network: https://unece.org/forests/team-specialists-forest-communication

43   Guidelines and tools for developing communication strategies: https://www.unaids.org/sites/default/files/media_asset/jc1582_guidelines_tools_en_3.pdf

The International Day of Forests encourages countries to organize activities involving forests and trees locally, nationally and internationally, such as:

- Tree-planting campaigns.
- Photo exhibits portraying the specific International Day theme for that year.
- Sharing infographics, videos, news and messages via social and other media.
- Wearing shirts with slogans that may draw the attention of people.
- Arranging seminars in schools, field trips, family picnics.
- Visiting beautiful, wooded places.
- Addressing the International Day at political summits and conferences.

The role of criteria and indicators in communicating forest-related topics

C&I for SFM may offer a framework for developing a communication strategy, focusing on clear messages that allow the public and policymakers to connect with issues and challenges, including information about the state of forests, forest management and the forest sector. C&I have emerged as a powerful tool to promote SFM as a result of the effective presentation of the economic, social and environmental benefits of forests. C&I can also spark dialogue with other sectors, and society at large, in developing a national forest programme. Moreover, C&I provide a means of presenting achievements in promoting SFM globally, regionally and nationally, as well as locally. Forests play a key role in supporting most of the SDGs, even though forests receive explicit mention in only two SDGs. Where national sets of C&I exist, they can support communication on how forests of national and regional scale contribute to sustainable livelihoods through income generation and employment, food production, resilient and sustainable production/consumption, and mitigating and adapting to climate change.

Policy implications

The forest sector must use widespread, continuous communication to respond to society on a broad range of social and environmental issues.

Devising a national forest policy requires systematic planning, and the use of forest-related communication strategies to convey succinct messages to well-targeted audiences.

National sets of C&I for SFM can present robust evidence on forests and their environmental and socioeconomic values nationally, regionally and internationally.

Given that the future of forests may depend as much, if not more, on public perception and expectations about forests than the efforts of foresters, communication will be a fundamental force to shape public opinion and to inform politicians.

The way forward

Public perception and expectations of forests have evolved in the last decades and now play an influential role in determining how forests are managed, affecting forest policymakers, forest owners and forest managers.

The challenges for forest communicators are to be attentive to society, and to explain the issues along with possibilities in forest management. This will lead to a better understanding of forestry and an appreciation of what shapes public opinion and the different values that forests provide.

The growing need for forest communication and improved public relations require a state-of-the-art approach, together with a new understanding and the skills to respond to the opportunities and challenges of reconciling competing views of forest management.

The criteria and indicators used for measuring SFM derive from environmental, social and economic forest functions and should help in communications with the wider community about the broad range of essential goods and services that forests provide.

River in Jeti Oguz valley, Kyrgyzstan

6. Conclusions

Over five years, the collective efforts of national key personnel and experts, international experts and the UNECE/FAO project team have enabled the five CCA countries to improve significantly their basis for monitoring, assessment and reporting of sustainable forest management, with the use C&I for SFM. Beginning from a common understanding of contemporary SFM and allowing participants to plan for the future, all five countries have successfully prepared final national C&I for SFM, accompanied by detailed factsheets for each indicator.

The participatory nature of the process and the different conditions in every country mean that national sets of C&I for SFM differ in content, structure and size, as would be expected. It is also expected that the national C&I for SFM sets will further evolve over time due to new emerging issues or additional capacity-building. The experience of implementation and improvements in monitoring will give a chance to further develop and optimize the national C&I sets.

The challenge ahead is to implement these C&I for the first time, which will require efficient monitoring, accurate assessment and comprehensive reporting on the progress of SFM. Setting up a database for reporting will contribute to improving standards of forest management at every stage of implementation. Most importantly, the process will foster national political discussions about SFM and forest-related issues like climate change adaptation, bioeconomy or biodiversity and help to include the interests of a wide range of stakeholders. This has been one of the successes of the interim workshop held in Tbilisi in 2018 and the final conference in Issyk Kul in 2019.

Monitoring, assessment and reporting of C&I have followed different approaches. Countries that have had a longer involvement in setting up C&I already have well-established systems for coordinating data collection and maintaining data in well-designed information systems. Such systems are able to produce a complex of analysis and reports addressing regular and ad-hoc demands. They are usually science-based, reporting information that has been gathered from monitoring. Databases and reports give comprehensive data tailored to the needs of intended audiences.

Limited resources, coupled with an unfavourable enabling environment, will result in challenges for CCA countries. At every phase of the process, CCA countries will need to simplify the C&I set to a level that can be implemented.

The project helped participants to tailor their national C&I sets to a national capacity for implementation. Therefore, it is expected that reliable data would be readily available, allowing countries to report with confidence based on their final national C&I for SFM sets. The factsheets prepared by

CCA countries are essential in setting out the rationales for the indicators; data sources; measurement units; periodicity of data availability; targets; thresholds; institutions which will collect, manage and use the data; reference to international reporting obligations; and related definitions.

A first step could be to involve setting up a national supervisory system to streamline the process of organizing, coordinating and facilitating data collection, monitoring and assessment of the C&I for SFM. Most CCA countries have considered assigning this role to the most relevant forestry unit. There could be a case for setting up, on a voluntary basis, a committee of national stakeholder representatives to oversee management of the process. This approach could even further enhance credibility and acceptance of the C&I for SFM. Government forestry units could act as the secretariat, handling procedures, providing logistic support and acting as facilitators.

Countries are likely to use official procedure to legitimize national C&I for SFM, through a regulation or decree. It is recommended that such a regulation or decree should define a structure and a coordinating committee, with a clear mandate to supervise and coordinate the whole process at the country level. Such a mandate may include roles and responsibilities of every unit involved in implementing C&I for SFM monitoring, assessing and reporting, with a calendar starting from the call for data collection through to assessment. Such a committee might also be able to set up participatory working groups, when necessary, for the pre-assessment of every criterion/indicator, once data have been collected.

Including a pre-assessment stage would be beneficial. Data need to be presented in a form that will be easily understood by outsiders, providing knowledge that will help policymakers and decision makers to reach informed decisions. With this approach, reporting could start from the first cycle of the process, when data are obtained for a particular indicator. The data provider could include a commentary setting out the reasons or underlying causes behind any trend and adding proposals to improve the situation. This could take the form of a "facts and figures" sheet, with additional information, allowing full interpretation of collected data. A table giving only raw data could lead to a wrong perception about the state of a certain indicator. For example, numbers for "growing stock" may show a significant decrease over the previous year, but this may be because of exceptional extreme weather with droughts and forest fire damages for that particular year and should not be seen as a trend.

A committee, or working groups set up by it, should review pre-assessments. Whether or not thresholds or targets exist, the ultimate opinion for a given indicator and eventually for a criterion should ideally be the result of agreement between committee members and compiled into a respective report. It may not be possible to achieve an agreement, in which case the committee should record disagreements and objections in its report.

A country should release a comprehensive, periodical national report (e.g. every five years). This can preferably be done through a national panel/workshop where panellists (focal points for each criterion) present the analysis of the related indicators under each criterion based on data collected and reports published within the last period. The results of discussions at broader level will yield a comprehensive national report on SFM in the country with recommendations and proposals addressed to all stakeholders and government to leverage additional resources for SFM.

Many indicators are linked to the SDGs and to the Global Core Set of Forest-related Indicators. If national C&I for SFM are developed in a comprehensive way, the related data collection should be able to meet the diverse and increasing reporting requirements of various processes and organizations, without much additional effort. Reporting the results to UNFF, FAO, UNECE or any other body that requires forest-related information should follow.

Implementing C&I for SFM at FMU level is vital to achieving SFM overall. Based on the premise that practical solutions to problems come from those working closest to them, there is a strong case for involving personnel at FMU level during implementation of C&I for SFM. Dealing with issues locally may improve communication, cooperation, collaboration and compromise between stakeholders; however, in many cases it would require additional effort in coordinating work between the national and local levels. National C&I for SFM are not directly applicable on FMU level, but if relevant they should be translated to the level of the FMU-related C&I for SFM and vice-versa when reported back to the national monitoring and assessment.

MAR on C&I for SFM is primarily done on a national level. As a consequence, aggregated information may cloud the diversity of situations, especially for indicators where reported values could vary geographically (e.g. regions) and thematically (e.g. species). Thus, it is essential the C&I for SFM and related data collection are able to identify and depict this diversity. Participation of stakeholders is one of the essential elements assisting in this identification and supporting related analytical and reporting work.

Quantitative and qualitative attributes of indicators should be presented in ways that shed light on the state of the various criteria and show how they relate to each other. Good quality data about the status of SFM are essential to support evidence-based policymaking. Individual countries will adapt and innovate in developing methods that better suit their particular circumstances.

Forest management plans play a key role in the C&I for SFM process. They are the backbone of forest management and information systems. They are the source of various data for indicators and also the primary tool for implementing SFM in the field. Improving countries' forest management planning systems merits special attention. Developing modern management planning systems, based on the results and experiences from these projects, should benefit all CCA countries.

Forest management plans cannot provide all the data for C&I for SFM and will therefore need to be supplemented by national forest inventories, field surveys, biodiversity-related observation systems and other data collection means. Establishing GIS systems, supported by data from remote sensing, including aerial photography, will help greatly. The cost of GIS and mapping systems has become more affordable in recent years. The key challenge will be to establish, run and maintain relevant institutions/systems, and to recruit and retain the qualified personnel. Forestry departments in the CCA countries should continue to strengthen their technical capacity and explore how to retain skilled personnel.

National C&I for SFM can work effectively as an information and communication tool. A problem raised throughout the workshops was that of weak coordination and collaboration between different sectors. This is not unique to the CCA countries. It is a common problem across the world and can impact directly forest sector development.

Well-designed information and communication strategies could galvanize better coordination and cooperation. Many CCA countries have already started to include goals in national forest programmes for raising awareness and improving perceptions about forests. Basing new forest-related strategies on assessment reports using C&I data is a good first step towards implementing SFM.

Step-by-Step

1. Set up a supervisory system

Data collection, monitoring, assessment and reporting on C&I for SFM should be organized in a comprehensive way and overseen by a supervisory body.

For most CCA countries, at first sight, it might seem convenient to assign such tasks to one of the existing forestry organizations. The process might benefit, and be more credible and effective, by having a coordinating committee of representatives of all stakeholders, established on a voluntary basis. The principal government forestry organization could act as secretariat, organizing the work, providing logistical support and acting as facilitator.

2. Create legal instruments

Most countries are likely to adopt official procedures for the approval of national C&I for SFM and incorporating them into legislation. When legislation is being drafted, they should identify supervisory bodies to oversee and coordinate the whole process at the national level and define their mandate.

3. Use factsheets as guidelines

The factsheets prepared by CCA countries significantly reduce the need to prepare implementation guidelines. Factsheets already lay out for every indicator the corresponding rationale, data sources, measurement units, periodicity of data availability, targets, thresholds, institutions which collect, manage and use the data, references to international reporting obligations, and related definitions.

4. Pre-assess collected data

Data providers should attach a concise pre-assessment to the data collected or coordinated. It is important that all data be presented in a form that can be understood easily by users outside of the forest sector.

5. Assess the data for every indicator under all criteria to prepare a short-term, regular report

A coordinating committee, or its sub-working group should examine pre-assessments before results are ultimately compiled in a short-term report, prepared on a regular basis (e.g. annually). When it has not been possible to resolve disagreements about data, the reports should record disagreements and objections.

6. Prepare national long-term reports

A national workshop, with broad stakeholder participation could validate the state of forests and forestry assessed against C&I and finalize long-term national SFM reports. The reports should contain recommendations and proposals addressed to all stakeholders, decision makers and government. The reports could support raising additional financial resources and capacities for comprehensive long-term SFM.

7. Involve stakeholders representing national, regional and local levels

A participatory process will help stakeholders to better understand C&I for SFM and implications of their application at the national, regional and local levels. This participation would stimulate debate around additional ways and means to solve the problems. This would contribute to forest conservation and SFM at regional and local levels with a better understanding of national perspectives and goals.

8. Improve the system for forest management planning

Forest management plans provide the backbone of data for C&I for SFM. They are also the primarily tool for a framework for management activities in the field. Forest management plans should encompass the whole range of benefits that forests provide, not simply wood production, but taking an ecosystem-based approach.

9. Establish an effective and affordable information system for data gathering

Forest management plans cannot provide all the necessary data for C&I for SFM They will need to be combined with national forest inventories, special field surveys, biodiversity-related observation systems and other data sources. An information system, using various tools and sources (GIS, databanks, remote-sensing, aerial photography), will be the most effective tool for collecting and managing most of the data.

10. Prepare an information and communication strategy

Assessments and findings of C&I for SFM reports should improve the understanding of forests and forestry and the objectives and work of related institutions or organizations dealing with issues like climate change, biodiversity or bioeconomy. Information should be presented to target audiences comprehensibly and at the right time.

Nurek Reservoir in Dushanbe in Tajikistan

REFERENCES

Adler, R.; Towne, N. (1978): Looking out/looking in (2nd ed.). New York: Holt, Rinehart and Winston.

Adriaanse, A. (1995): In Search of Balance. A Conceptual Framework for Sustainable Development Indicators. In MacGillivray, A. (ed.) 1994. Accounting for Change. Papers from an International Seminar. Toynbee Hall. The New Economics Foundation. London. Pp. 3-10.

Aleinikov, A.V.; Mal'tseva, D.A.; Miletskii, V.P. (2016): Information and Information Technologies as Applied in Political Strategy Modeling. Scientific and Technical Information Processing 43, no. 2 (2016): 106–14. https://doi.org/10.3103/S0147688216020076

Avgerou, C. (2008): 'Information Systems in Developing Countries: A Critical Research Review'. Journal of Information Technology 23, no. 3/2008: 133–46. https://doi.org/10.1057/palgrave.jit.2000136

Brundtland, G.H. (1987): Our Common Future. [Brundtland-Report]. World Commission on Environment and Development (ed.). Oxford University Press. Oxford. 400 p.

COFO (2012): See list of meeting documents of the Committee on Forestry 2012

Cubbage, F.W.; O'Laughlin, J.; Bullock, C.S. (1993): Forest Resource Policy. John Wiley & Sons.

Dzebo A., Janetschek H., Brandi C. and Iacobuta G. (2019): Exploring connections between the Paris Agreement and the 2030 Agenda for Sustainable Development. Policy Brief. Stockholm Environment Institute. Stockholm, Sweden.

EC DG DEVCO Evaluation Unit (2020): Cost-Effectiveness Analysis. Capacity4dev. Accessed 26 October 2020. https://europa.eu/capacity4dev/evaluation_guidelines/wiki/cost-effectiveness-analysis-0

EFI (2013): Implementing Criteria and Indicators for Sustainable Forest Management in Europe. European Forest Institute: Joensuu, Finland. ISBN 978-952-5980-04-2 http://www.efi.int/sites/default/files/files/publication-bank/projects/efi_c-i_report_implementing_criteria_net_final.pdf

FAO (2003): Key issues in the future development of international initiatives on forest-related criteria and indicators for sustainable development – background paper 4. Report- International Conference on the Contribution of Criteria and Indicators for Sustainable Forest Management: The Way Forward (CICI-2003), Vol. 2 CICI – 2003 3 - 7 February 2003, Guatemala City, Guatemala

FAO (2011): Strengthening Monitoring, Assessment and Reporting on Sustainable Forest Management (GCP/INT/988/JPN). Technical Synthesis Report.

FAO (2015a): Criteria and indicators for sustainable forest management. Project website.

FAO (2015b): Global Forest Resources Assessment 2015. How are the world's forests changing? Second edition. FAO, Rome, http://www.fao.org/3/a-i4793e.pdf

FAO (2017): Keeping an eye on SDG 15. Working with countries to measure indicators for forests and mountains. FAO, Rome, 13 S. http://www.fao.org/3/a-i7334e.pdf

FAO (2018): Accelerating progress towards SDG 15. Secretariat Note. Committee on Forestry. Twenty-fourth session, Rome, 16-20 July 218. FO:COFO/218/5.1 http://www.fao.org/3/MW547EN/mw547en.pdf

FAO (2020): Global Forest Resources Assessment 2020. Main report. Rome. https://doi.org/10.4060/ca9825en

Forest Europe; UNECE; FAO (2011): State of Europe's Forests 2011; Status and Trends in Sustainable Forest Management in Europe; Forest Europe Liaison Unit: Oslo, Norway, 2011; ISBN 978-82-92980-05-7.

Giuntoli, J.; Robert, N.; Ronzon, T.; Sanchez Lopez, J.; Follador, M.; Girardi, I.; Barredo Cano, J.; Borzacchiello, M.; Sala, S.; M'Barek, R.; La Notte, A.; Becker, W.; Mubareka, S. (2020): Building a monitoring system for the EU bioeconomy, EUR 30064 EN, Publications Office of the European Union, Luxembourg, 2020, ISBN 978-92-76-15385-6.

Köhl, M., Magnussen, S. (2016): Sampling in Forest Inventories, in: Pancel, L., Köhl, M. (eds.): Tropical Forestry Handbook, Vol. 1, Springer, Heidelberg, 777-837

Köhl, M., Marchetti, M. (2016): Objectives and Planning of Forest Inventories, in: Pancel, L., Köhl, M. (eds.): Tropical Forestry Handbook, Vol. 1, Springer, Heidelberg, 749-776

Köhl, M.; Linser, S.; Prins, K. (Eds.) (2020): State of Europe's Forests 2020. Ministerial Conference on the Protection of Forests in Europe. Forest Europe Liaison Unit Bratislava, Slovakia.

Krause T. and Nielsen M.R. (2019): Not seeing the forest for the trees: the oversight of defaunation in REDD+ and global forest governance. Forests, 10(4), p.344.

Larman, C. (2004): Agile and Iterative Development: A Manager's Guide. Addison-Wesley Professional.

Linkevičius, E.; Borges, J.G.; Doyle, M.; Pülzl, H.; Nordström, E.-M.; Vacik, H.; Brukas, V. *et al.* (2019): Linking Forest Policy Issues and Decision Support Tools in Europe. Forest Policy and Economics 103 (June 2019): 4–16. https://doi.org/10.1016/j.forpol.2018.05.014

Lier, M.; Köhl, M.; Korhonen, K.; Linser, S.; Prins, K. (2021): Forest relevant targets in EU policy instruments - can progress be measured by the pan-European criteria and indicators for sustainable forest management? Forest Policy and Economics 128, 102481. https://doi.org/10.1016/j.forpol.2021.102481

Linser, S.; Wolfslehner, B. (2021): National implementation of the Forest Europe indicators for sustainable forest management. Draft submitted to Silva Fennica.

Linser, S.; Wolfslehner, B.; Gritten, D.; Rasi, R.; Johnson, S.; Bridge, S.; Payn, T.; Prins, K.; Robertson, G. (2018 a): 25 Years of Criteria and Indicators for Sustainable Forest Management - Have they made a difference? Forests 2018, 9(9), 578. https://doi.org/10.3390/f9090578

Linser, S.; Wolfslehner, B.; Asmar, F.; Bridge, S.R.J.; Gritten, D.; Guadalupe, V.; Jafari, M.; Johnson, S.; Laclau, P.; Robertson, G. (2018 b): 25 Years of Criteria and Indicators for Sustainable Forest Management: Why Some Intergovernmental C&I Processes Flourished While Others Faded. Forests 2018, 9 (9), 515. https://doi.org/10.3390/f9090515

Linser, S. (2020): Indikatoren für nachhaltige Waldbewirtschaftung 2020/ Austrian Indicators for Sustainable Forest Management 2020. Bundesministerium für Landwirtschaft, Regionen und Tourismus - BMLRT, Vienna, Austria, 290 p.

Linser, S.; Lier, M. (2020): The Contribution of Sustainable Development Goals and Forest-Related Indicators to National Bioeconomy Progress Monitoring. Sustainability 12(7):2898. https://doi.org/10.3390/su12072898

MCPFE (1993): Ministerial Conference on the Protection of Forests in Europe, 16-17 June 1993 in Helsinki.

MCPFE (1998): Third Ministerial Conference on the Protection of Forests in Europe. General declaration and resolutions adopted. Resolution L 2. Liaison Unit in Lisbon (Ed.).

Moss, L.T.; Atre, S. (2003): Business Intelligence Roadmap: The Complete Project Lifecycle for Decision-Support Applications. Addison-Wesley Professional.

Onida, M. (2021): Forest and forest policy between the EU and its Member States. ELNI Review. Environmental Law Network International, February 2021, pp. 22-30.

Ott, W. (1978): Environmental Indices: Theory and Practice. Ann Arbour Science. Ann Arbour. 371 p.

Rauscher, H.M.; Schmoldt, D.L.; Vacik, H. (2007): Information and Knowledge Management in Support of Sustainable Forestry: A Review. In Sustainable Forestry: From Monitoring and Modelling to Knowledge Management and Policy Science, edited by K. M. Reynolds, A. J. Thomson, M. Köhl, M. A. Shannon, D. Ray, and K. Rennolls, 439–60. Wallingford: CABI, 2007. https://doi.org/10.1079/9781845931742.0439

Rayner, J.; Buck, A.; Katila, P.; Cashore, B.; Hoogeveen, H.; Verkooijen, P.V.J.D.; Wood, P.; Arts, B.J.M.; Visseren-Hamakers, I.J. (2010): Embracing complexity in international forest governance: a way forward. Eds.; IUFRO World Series; IUFRO: Vienna, Austria, 2010; Volume 28, ISBN 978-3-902762-01-6.

Schanz, H. (1996): 'Forstliche Nachhaltigkeit' - Sozialwissenschaftliche Analyse der Begriffsinhalte und –funktionen [Sustainable Forest Management – contents and functions of a central term in a social science perspective]. Dissertation Universität Freiburg. Schriften des Instituts für Forstökonomie, Band IV. Freiburg. 131 p., in German.

Sommer, J.M. (2020): Global governance in forestry: a cross-national analysis. International Journal of Sustainable Development & World Ecology, pp.1-15.

Sotirov, M., Pokorny, B., Kleinschmit, D. and Kanowski P. (2020): International Forest Governance and Policy: Institutional Architecture and Pathways of Influence in Global Sustainability. Sustainability, 12(17), p.7010.

Tegegne, Y.T., Cramm, M. and Van Brusselen, J. (2018): Sustainable forest management, FLEGT, and REDD+: Exploring interlinkages to strengthen forest policy coherence. Sustainability, 10(12), p.4841.

The Montréal Process (2015): The Montréal Process Criteria and Indicators for the Conservation and Sustainable Management of Temperate and Boreal Forests.5th Ed. Montréal Process Liaison Office: https://www.montrealprocess.org/

Thomson, A.J., Rauscher, H.M., Schmoldt, D.L., Vacik, H (2007): Information and Knowledge Management for Sustainable Forestry. In Sustainable Forestry: From Monitoring and Modelling to Knowledge Management and Policy Science, edited by K.

M. Reynolds, A. J. Thomson, M. Köhl, M. A. Shannon, D. Ray, and K. Rennolls, 374–92. Wallingford: CABI, 2007. https://doi.org/10.1079/9781845931742.0374

Tomppo, E., Gschwantner, Th., Lawrence, M., McRoberts, R.E. (Eds.) (2020): National Forest Inventories, Springer, Heidelberg

UN (1973): Report of the United Nations Conference on the Human Environment, Stockholm, 5-16 June 1972. A/CONF.48/14/Rev.1. United Nations, New York.

UN (1992): The Rio Declaration on Environment and Development. UN Conference on Environment and Development, Rio de Janeiro: UN, 13 June 1992.A/CONF.151/5/Rev.1. United Nations, New York.

UN (1997): Agenda 21: Programme of Action for Sustainable Development: Rio Declaration on Environment and Development: Statement of Forest Principles. [ST/]DPI/1344/Rev.1/SD. United Nations, New York. 294 p.

UN (2007a): Non-legally binding instrument on all types of forests: note / by the Secretariat. A/RES/62/98. United Nations, New York.

UN (2007b): Indicators of Sustainable Development: Guidelines and Methodologies. United Nations publication Sales No. E.08. II.A.2 ISBN 978-92-1-104577-2.

UN (2017): United Nations Strategic Plan for Forests 2017-2030 and quadrennial programme of work of the United Nations Forum on Forests for the period 2017-2020: resolution / adopted by the Economic and Social Council. E/RES/2017/4. UN. Economic and Social Council 2016-2017: New York and Geneva.

UN (2018): United Nations Forest Instrument. Available online: https://www.un.org/esa/forests/wp-content/uploads/2018/08/UN_Forest_Instrument.pdf

UNCED (1993): Report of the United Nations Conference on Environment and Development. Rio de Janeiro, 3-14 June 1992. A/CONF.151/26/Rev. I (Vol. I) United Nations publication No. E.93.1.8.

UNECE/FAO (2016): Pilot Project on the System for the Evaluation of the Management of Forests (SEMAFOR). Geneva Timber and Forest Discussion Paper 66. ECE/TIM/DP/66, (ed. Prins, K.). United Nations, New York and Geneva, 167 p. ISBN: 978-92-1-117123-5

UNECE/FAO (2019a): State of Forests of the Caucasus and Central Asia. ECE/TIM/SP/47, (ed. Prins, K.). United Nations, New York and Geneva, 121 p. ISBN 978-92-1-117198-3

UNECE/FAO (2019b): Guidelines for the Development of a Criteria and Indicator Set for Sustainable Forest Management. ECE/TIM/DP/73, (ed. Linser, S.; O'Hara, P.) United Nations, New York and Geneva, 89 p. https://doi.org/10.13140/RG.2.2.32430.36168/1

Vacik, H.; Wolfslehner, B.; Seidl, R.; Lexer, M.J. (2007): Integrating the DPSIR Approach and the Analytic Network Process for the Assessment of Forest Management Strategies. Sustainable Forestry: From Monitoring and Modelling to Knowledge Management and Policy Science, 2007, 393–411.

Vidal, C., Alberdi, I., Hernández, L., Redmond, J.J. (Eds.) (2016): National Forest Inventories – Assessment of Wood Availability and Use, Springer, Heidelberg

Wolfslehner, B.; Linser, S.; Pülzl, H.; Bastrup-Birk, A.; Camia, A.; Marchetti, M. Forest Bioeconomy—A New Scope for Sustainability Indicators; From Science to Policy 4; European Forest Institute: Joensuu, Finland, 2016, ISBN 978-952-5980-29-5. https://doi.org/10.36333/fs04

The following reports served as background information for the elaboration of this study:

Report of Regional Inception Workshop on C&I for SFM in CCA Region, A.K. Coker, T. Loeffler with input from S. Linser, P. O'Hara, R. Michalak, Armenia, 2016

Report of the 2nd National Workshop on C&I for SFM for Armenia, Y. Danielyan, 2019

Report of the 2nd National Workshop on C&I for SFM for Georgia, G. Aleksidze, 2018

Report of the 2nd National Workshop on C&I for SFM for Kyrgyzstan, S. Seideeva, 2018

Report of the 2nd National Workshop on C&I for SFM for Uzbekistan, A. Zakhadullaev, 2018

Report of the 2nd National Workshop on C&I for SFM in Kazakhstan, N. Raimkulov, 2018

Report of the National Coaching Workshop on C&I for SFM for Georgia, G. Aleksidze, 2017

Report of the National Coaching Workshop on C&I for SFM for Kyrgyzstan, S. Seideeva, 2017

Report of the National Coaching Workshop on C&I for SFM for Uzbekistan, A. Zakhadullaev, 2017

Report of the National Coaching Workshop on C&I for SFM in Kazakhstan, N. Raimkulov, 2017

Report of the Regional Interim Workshop on C&I for SFM in CCA Region, R. Shelest, UNECE/FAO, Georgia, 2018

Report of the Forestry Congress for the Caucasus and Central Asia, R. Shelest, UNECE/FAO, 2019

Organizations with expertise in Monitoring, Assessment and Reporting

The FAO offers information on MAR on its website under "Assessment and monitoring" (http://www.fao.org/forestry/en/). Particularly relevant are:

- An assessment of forest resources (http://www.fao.org/forest-resources-assessment/en/), including the recent FRA-2020.
- Information on forest monitoring and assessment (http://www.fao.org/forestry/fma/en/). This page is also linked to the Voluntary Guidelines for National Forest Monitoring (http://www.fao.org/forestry/fma/84322/en/).
- Information on C&I for SFM (http://www.fao.org/forestry/ci/en/).
- Practical guidelines for the MAR on national-level criteria and indicators that have been developed for different regions (e.g. for the dry forests of Asia) (http://www.fao.org/3/ap160e/ap160e.pdf).
- The development of MAR for the Asia and Pacific Region (http://www.fao.org/forestry/mar/en/).
- The Technical Synthesis Report on "Strengthening Monitoring, Assessment and Reporting on Sustainable Forest Management" (GCP/INT/988/JPN)", (http://www.apafri.org/publications/MAR%20Report.pdf).
- National Forest Monitoring and Assessment – Manual for integrated field data collection (http://www.fao.org/forestry/14727-072b68bcfa49334202f1586889517ce24.pdf).
- The Open Foris is an FAO-led initiative to develop, share and support specialized software tools required by countries and institutions to implement multi-purpose forest inventories (https://openforis.org/).

International sources/organizations with expertise in outreach on forest-related issues

The UNECE-FAO Forest Communicators Network: https://unece.org/forests/team-specialists-forest-communication

Forest communication toolkits: http://www.fao.org/forestry/communication-toolkit/76361/en/

Best Practices in Forest Communication UNECE-FAO Forest Communicators Network http://www.fao.org/forestry/communication-toolkit/76358/en/

Global Coordination Group of the Regional Forest Communicators Network: More information available here: http://www.fao.org/forestry/communication-toolkit/87164/en/

UN International Day of Forests: https://www.un.org/en/observances/forests-and-trees-day; http://www.fao.org/international-day-of-forests/en/

Other recommended communication related reading

Communication cycle: Definition, process, models and examples: https://studylib.net/doc/8076219/communication-cycle--definition--process--models-and

Communication- A Systematic Process https://www.bartleby.com/essay/Communication-A-Systematic-Process-F3QSS94CDM6S

The Role of Communication in Social Forestry: https://www.researchgate.net/publication/43090918_The_Role_of_Communication_in_Social_Forestry_The_Case_of_Mwenezi

Best Practices in Slovak Forestry Communication – case study, Marusakova, L. (2009): Forestry Journal 55(4), DOI: 10.2478/v110114-009-0009-0.

Lake Kaindy in Kazakhstan

ANNEX: National Criteria and Indicators for Sustainable Forest Management

ARMENIA - 7 Criteria and 43 indicators

Criterion 1

Maintenance and enhancement of the forest area in Armenia

1.1 Total area of forest cover

1.2 Forest area as a proportion of total land area

1.3 Area of forests classified by main special-purpose significance

1.4 Area of forest managed based on actual management plans

1.5 Area of forest cover in specially protected areas of nature

1.6 Forest cover changes observed in forested areas

1.7 Planted forest area on non-forested lands

1.8 Forest area changes due to the changes in the land purpose

1.9 Annual changes in the operational significance of forest lands

1.10 Survival rate of afforestation/reforestation

1.11 Number of recorded illegal loggings

Criterion 2:

Maintenance of the biodiversity in Armenia's forests

2.1 Species diversity

2.2 Endemic species

2.3 Invasive species

2.4 Threatened forest species classified according to IUCN National Red List

2.5 Natural regeneration of forest

2.6 Activities carried out to support natural regeneration of forests

Criterion 3

Maintenance of health and vitality in Armenia's forest

3.1 Forest area damaged by pests, diseases, and fires

3.2 Forest area affected directly by human activities

Criterion 4

Maintenance of the productive functions of Armenia's forest resources

4.1 Mean increment of forests

4.2 Volume and area of fellings

4.3 Number of tree seedlings in (state) nurseries, reported by tree species

4.4 Share of wood-based energy in total energy consumption

Criterion 5

Maintenance of the protective functions of Armenia's forests

5.1 Area of forest cover in watersheds

Criterion 6

Maintenance of the socio-economic functions of Armenia's forest resources

6.1 Volume of import and export of timber and wood products

6.2 Financial revenues of forest enterprises generated from sales of non-wood and secondary forest products

6.3 The dynamics of the sales of non-timber products according to the forest coupons

6.4 Revenues from the paid services of forests and other forest lands

6.5 Forest sector workforce

6.6 Average salary of employees in the "Hayantar" SNCO

6.7 Occupational health and safety of forest workers

6.8 Dissemination of the environmental awareness raising programs in forest-neighboring communities

Criterion 7

Legal, policy and institutional framework for a sustainable management of Armenia's forests

7.1 Forest strategic policy and National Forest Programme

7.2 Annual forest monitoring programs and reports

7.3 The ratio of the number of forest enterprises with a current forest management plan to the total number of forest enterprises

7.4 Performance and reporting on international obligations

7.5 Public participation in the discussions on drafting legal acts on forest sector

7.6 National, international, and other funding committees to SFM

7.7 Taxation, financial and economic instruments supporting the sustainable management of forests

7.8 Presence of forest and forest land cadaster

7.9 Innovative technologies in forest sector

7.10 The quantity and titles of research works related to first sector in universities and research institutes

7.11 Number of graduate students of ANAU "Forestry and landscape gardening program" (bachelor, master, doctorate)

GEORGIA - 14 Criteria, 43 indicators, 37 sub-indicators

Criterion 1

The area covered by forest in Georgia is maintained

1.1 Area of forests

    1.1.1 Total forest area

    1.1.2 Forest area as proportion of total land area

    1.1.3 Forest area annual net change rate

1.2 Area of different forest categories

    1.2.1 Forest area available for wood supply = commercial forest

    1.2.2 Protected forest areas (including Emerald Sites)

    1.2.3 Primary forest area = forest area undisturbed by man

    1.2.4 Protective forest area

    1.2.5 Recreation forest area

1.2.6 Area and proportion of forest under long-term forest management plans, which are approved by the responsible Ministry

Criterion 2

The natural biodiversity of the forests in Georgia is maintained and enhanced

2.1 Total forest area by stand origin

    2.1.1 Naturally regenerated forest area

    2.1.2 Planted forest area

2.2 Tree species composition and abundance

    2.2.1 Tree species composition/diversity

    2.2.2 Abundance/frequency of endemic tree species

    2.2.3 Abundance/frequency of introduced tree species and share of invasive tree species

    2.2.4 Abundance/frequency of endangered tree species / red list tree species

2.3 Structure of forest stands classified according to number of layers (vertical structure) and stem distribution (horizontal structure)

2.4 Abundance/frequency of habitat trees

2.5 Volume of standing and down deadwood in forest

    2.5.1 Standing dead wood

    2.5.2 Down dead wood

2.6 Area of old-growth forests

Criterion 3

The vitality of the forests in Georgia is maintained and enhanced ensuring the protective functions of the forest

3.1 Regeneration capacity of forest stands classified by different tree species, height classes, damage, and health

3.2 Forest damage by abiotic, biotic, and anthropogenic causes classified by different tree species, causes and severity of damage

3.3 Forest land degradation classified by reason and severity of degradation

Criterion 4

The productivity of Georgia's forest is enhanced

4.1 Growing stock of wood, classified by   forest type and by availability for wood supply

    4.1.1 Growing stock on forest land, classified by availability for wood supply and by tree species: coniferous and broadleaved.

    4.1.2 Growing stock by forest type: coniferous, broadleaved, and mixed forests

    4.1.3 Growing stock composition, classified by main species

4.2 Increment of wood classified by tree species

4.3 Age structure and/or diameter distribution of forest, classified by forest type and by availability for wood supply

    4.3.1 Age class distribution (area of even-aged stands) classified by forest type

4.3.2 Age class distribution (volume of even-aged stands) in forest available for wood supply classified by forest type

4.3.3 Diameter distribution and total area (uneven-aged stands)

Criterion 5

The contribution of the Georgian Forests to the Carbon Cycles is enhanced

5.1 Carbon stock in litter, dead wood, soil above ground and below-ground biomass

    5.1.1 Carbon stock in growing stock

    5.1.2 Carbon stock in below-ground biomass

    5.1.3 Carbon stock in litter

    5.1.4 Carbon stock in dead wood (down dead wood, standing dead wood

    5.1.5 Carbon stock in soil

5.2 Carbon stock in harvested wood resources

    5.2.1 Carbon stock in harvested wood products

    5.2.2 Share of wood-based energy in total primary energy supply

Criterion 6

The productive function of Georgia's forests is maintained on a sustainable level

6.1 Total volume legally and illegally harvested wood and wood from unplanned incidents compared with increment (see indicator 4.2) classified by tree species

    6.1.1 Volume of legally harvested wood classified by tree species and quality

    6.1.2 Volume of wood damaged by abiotic and biotic damaging agents

    6.1.3 Volume of illegally harvested wood classified by tree species and quality

6.2 Value of roundwood (including Industrial and fuel wood) legally and illegally obtained from forests

6.3 Consumption of wood (including fuelwood) and products derived from wood

6.4 Imports and exports of wood (including fuel wood) and products derived from wood

Criterion 7

The processing of timber in Georgia is promoted

7.1 Number, territorial distribution and operating capacity of sawmills, classified by legally and illegally operating sawmills

7.2 Number, territorial distribution and operating capacity of secondary wood processing facilities (e.g. carpentries, enterprises) classified by legally and illegally operating facilities

Criterion 8

The contribution of the forest sector to the Georgian economy is increased on a sustainable basis and acknowledged

8.1 Contribution of the forest sector to the GDP classified by:
- Wood products.
- Non-wood Forest Products.
- Marketed Services (see indicator 10.1)

8.2 Financial resources for the implementation of sustainable forest management

    8.2.1 State budget allocated for forest sector institutions responsible for policy, regulatory, monitoring and supervision tasks (e.g. BFD/FPD and DES/forest sector related supervision)

    8.2.2 State budget allocated for forest management bodies classified by:
- Total budget.
- % of budget for forest operations (including, road construction and maintenance, forest use – harvesting of wood, supplying fuelwood to schools and budgetary organizations).
- % of budget for forest restoration and maintenance.
- % of budget for forest management planning.
- % of budget for administration costs (including salaries of staff).

    8.2.3 Share of state budget allocated for the forest sector (8.2.1 + 8.2.2) in total state budget

    8.2.4 Support of donors for the forest sector

8.3 Net revenue of public forest management bodies (e.g. NFA, Ajara Forest Agency, APA, Akhmeta municipality, etc.)

8.4 Financial loss induced by illegal use of forest

Criterion 9

The use of Non-wood Forest Products (NWFPs) for commercial purposes and Marketed services provided by Georgian forests are enhanced without compromising other ecosystem services and functions of the forest

9.1 Quantity and market value of non-wood forest products

9.2 Quantity of marketed non-wood forest products compared with identified sustainable amounts specified in the license contract

9.3 Value of marketed services from forest

Criterion 10

Working conditions in the forest sector are "decent" and staff employed in the forest sector has adequate qualification

10.1 Employees in the forest sector on different levels (central, regional, district) classified by gender, age group, education, and position

10.2 Fatal and non-fatal occupational accidents and occupational diseases classified by type of work and seriousness of accidents

10.3 Average hourly earnings of female and male employees, by occupation, age, and persons with disabilities.

10.4 On-the-job-training for employees of forest management and supervisory bodies as well as private companies and license holders to gain the required certificates classified by subjects

Criterion 11

Forest education is improved

11.1 Number of graduates of forestry and related programs classified by the obtained degree and qualification

11.2 Access to forestry education and trainings for rural population

Criterion 12

Income opportunities for rural population are created

12.1 NWFP utilization licenses for rural population classified by individual Non-wood Forest Products

12.2 Wood supply for legal sawmills and carpentries in rural areas classified by tree species and wood qualities

12.3 Income opportunities in the tourism sector for rural population

12.4 Number rural population legally employed in forest operations

Criterion 13

Everybody's access to forests is ensured

13.1 The use of forests for recreation in terms of right of access, provision of facilities and intensity of use

13.2 Average grazing areas and the distance between 'grazing areas for common use' and 'settlements'

Criterion 14

Dissemination of the information and stakeholders participate in planning and decision-making process pertaining forest management is ensured

14.1 Stakeholder participation in forest management planning and decision making

14.2 Effective system for disseminating public information about SFM in Georgia

KAZAKHSTAN - 4 Criteria, 13 Indicators

Criterion 1

Biodiversity conservation

1.1 Forest area by geographic location (mountain forests, desert forests, floodplain forests, riparian forests, split forests, Kazakh hummocks, belt pine forests, island pine forests) and their percentage of the total forest fund area

1.2 Forest area of specially protected natural areas and their percentage of the total area of protected areas

1.3 Distribution of areas of the state forest fund by main forest-forming species

Criterion 2

Maintaining the productive capacity of forest ecosystems

2.1 Total timber stock in forests

2.2 The area and stock of timber of a private forest fund

2.3 The volume of annual timber harvesting in the context of all types of forest felling

2.4 Annual volume of harvesting of non-timber forest resources (secondary use)

Criterion 3

Protection of forests from fire, pests and diseases

3.1 The area of forests infected with pests, forest diseases, including invasive species

3.2 Forest area covered by forest fires

Criterion 4

Maintaining and expanding long-term multiple socio-economic benefits to meet the needs of society

4.1 Capital investment and annual expenditure on forestry, timber and non-timber forest products, environmental services, recreation, and tourism

4.2 Annual investments and expenditures from the state budget: a) for research on forestry, b) for education

4.3 Forest area and proportion available and/or managed for recreation and tourism

4.4 Cost and number of visits in the state forest fund related to recreation and tourism

---

KYRGYZSTAN - 6 Criteria, 54 Indicators, 4 Sub-Indicators

Criterion 1

Maintenance and enhancement of the forest ecosystems and forest resources conditions

1.1 Forest area and its proportion of total land use

1.2. The area of plantations and its proportion of the total forest area

1.3 Forest area designated for exploitation (recreation, tourism, forestry activities) and its proportion of the total forest area

1.4 The areas of forest lands transferred to leasehold use, including the proportion covered by forests and the number of forest leasehold users

1.5 Changes in the areas of forest pastures

1.6 Areas of stable plantations to the total area of forests (for Leshozes based on forest inventory materials)

1.7 Forests area by forest types and other characteristics

1.8 The area of forests affected by climatic and anthropogenic factors

1.9 The areas of settlements in the area of the state forest fund and in protected forest areas

Criterion 2

Conservation and maintenance of forest biodiversity

2.1 Forest area change in specially protected natural areas, State Forest Fund and area designated for creation of specially protected natural territories

2.2 Forests area with particularly valuable wood and shrub species and its proportion in the total forest area

2.3 Expenses for scientific research for the conservation of biodiversity

2.4 Forest area designated to preserve or maintain the genetic diversity of forests

2.5 Funds allocated for biotechnical activities

2.6 Forest area susceptible to diseases and pests

2.7 High conservation value forest area

Criterion 3

Maintenance and increase of forest productivity

3.1 The proportion of forest land for which there is a long-term forest management plan

3.2 Stocks of wood by species

3.3 Increment and fellings

3.4 Non-timber forest products, including wild medicinal plants, fruit products, mushrooms, honey, technical raw materials, and game

3.5 Annual volume of afforestation and reforestation

3.6 Fellings from industrial plantations

3.7 Pasture use

3.8 Number of forest management plans

3.9 Permissions for grazing

3.10 Number of forest reserves

3.11 Forest farms where integrated management is carried out

Criterion 4

Increasing the socio-economic importance of forests

4.1 The contribution of forestry to the gross national product

4.2 Investments directed to the forest industry

4.3 Permanently residents on the territory of the forest fund

4.4 Open positions at forestry enterprises

4.5 The population that receives income from the forest

4.6 State budget allocations directed to the forest industry

4.7 Development of alternative sources of income for the local population

4.8 Certified forests areas according to international standards

4.9 Number of rental agreements

4.11 Number of contracts for the creation of plantations

4.12 Technical support

4.13 Proportion of forest users who submit statistical reports "2X-forest user"

Criterion 5

Political, legislative, and institutional framework for sustainable forest management

5.1 National forest policy and legislative framework

5.2 Improvement of the organizational structure of State agency for environmental protection and forestry and its subordinate organizations

5.3 Financial and economic instruments in the field of sustainable forest management

    5.3.1 Payments for ecosystem services

5.4 Collaboration with Scientific Institutions for Sustainable Forest Management

5.5 Development of research and implementation of scientific developments and technologies

    5.5.1 Data for the assessment of ecosystem services for forests (may be a criterion for biodiversity

5.6 Development of human resources

    5.6.1 Increased skills and knowledge

    5.6.2 Age structure of forestry workers

5.7 Participation of stakeholders in the development and implementation of forest policy

5.8 International cooperation in the field of forest relations

5.9 Monitoring, evaluation and reporting on the management and development of the forest sector

5.10 Dissemination of information on forestry

5.11 Established forestry information system

Criterion 6

Improvement of social status of forestry workers

6.1 Average salaries of forestry workers

6.2 Social benefits

6.3 Improvement of infrastructure

UZBEKISTAN - 7 Criteria, 28 Indicators

Criterion 1

Extent of forest resources and global carbon cycle

1.1 Policies, institutions, and instruments to maintain and appropriately enhance forest resources and their contribution to the global carbon cycles

1.2 Area of forests and the area of other wooded land and as proportion of total land area

1.3 Forest area dedicated to the provision of specialized services

1.4 Growing stock on forest and other wooded land

1.5 Carbon stock and carbon stock changes

Criterion 2

Forest ecosystem health and vitality

2.1 Policies, institutions, and instruments to maintain forest ecosystem health and vitality

2.2 Forest damage

2.3 Forest land degradation

2.4 Rehabilitated and reforested forest area

Criterion 3

Biological diversity in forest ecosystems

3.1 Policies, institutions, and instruments to maintain, conserve and appropriately enhance the biological diversity in forest ecosystems

3.2 Area of planted forests

3.3 Number of introduced tree species

3.4 Protected forest areas and their proportion in designated natural territories.

Criterion 4

Productive functions of forests

4.1 Policies, institutions, and instruments to maintain and encourage the productive functions of forests

4.2 Rate of conversion of forests to non-forestry land uses

4.3 Production of non-wood forest products

4.4 Wood production

4.5 Seed resources

Criterion 5

Forest management plan

5.1 Policies, institutions, and instruments to improve the sustainable management of forests

5.2 Percentage of forests/other wooded lands managed according to management plans

5.3 Forest fire security roads and strips

5.4 Number of allowed livestock in the State Forest Fund's forest pasture lands

Criterion 6

Protective functions of forests

6.1 Policies, institutions, and instruments to maintain and appropriately enhance the protective functions of Uzbekistan's forests

6.2 Soil conditions

Criterion 7

Socio-economic functions and conditions

7.1 Policies, institutions, and instruments to maintain other socio-economic functions and conditions

7.2 Forest sector workforce

7.3 Economic contribution of the forest sector to the GDP

7.4 Investments in forests and forestry

INFORMATION ABOUT THE COMMITTEE ON FORESTS AND THE FOREST INDUSTRY

The UNECE Committee on Forests and the Forest Industry is a principal subsidiary body of the UNECE (United Nations Economic Commission for Europe) based in Geneva. It constitutes a forum for cooperation and consultation between member countries on forestry, the forest industry and forest product matters. All countries of Europe, the Commonwealth of Independent States, the United States of America, Canada and Israel are members of the UNECE and participate in its work.

The UNECE Committee on Forests and the Forest Industry shall, within the context of sustainable development, provide member countries with the information and services needed for policymaking and decision-making with regard to their forest and forest industry sectors, including the trade and use of forest products and, where appropriate, will formulate recommendations addressed to member governments and interested organizations. To this end, it shall:

1. With the active participation of member countries, undertake short-, medium- and long-term analyses of developments in, and having an impact on, the sector, including those developments offering possibilities for the facilitation of international trade and for enhancing the protection of the environment;

2. In support of these analyses, collect, store and disseminate statistics relating to the sector, and carry out activities to improve their quality and comparability;

3. Provide the framework for cooperation e.g. by organizing seminars, workshops and ad hoc meetings and setting up time limited ad hoc groups, for the exchange of economic, environmental and technical information between governments and other institutions of member countries required for the development and implementation of policies leading to the sustainable development of the sector and to the protection of the environment in their respective countries;

4. Carry out tasks identified by the UNECE or the Committee on Forests and the Forest Industry as being of priority, including the facilitation of subregional cooperation and activities in support of the economies in transition of central and eastern Europe and of the countries of the region that are developing from an economic perspective;

5. It should also keep under review its structure and priorities and cooperate with other international and intergovernmental organizations active in the sector, and in particular with the FAO (the Food and Agriculture Organization of the United Nations) and its European Forestry Commission, and with the ILO (the International Labour Organization), in order to ensure complementarity and to avoid duplication, thereby optimizing the use of resources.

More information about the Committee's work may be obtained by contacting:

UNECE/FAO Forestry and Timber Section

Forests, Land and Housing Division

United Nations Economic Commission for Europe/

Food and Agriculture Organization of the United Nations

Palais des Nations

CH-1211 Geneva 10, Switzerland

info.ECE-FAOforests@un.org

www.unece.org/forests

SOME FACTS ABOUT THE EUROPEAN FORESTRY COMMISSION

The European Forestry Commission (EFC) was created in 1947 and it is one of six Regional Forestry Commissions established by FAO to provide a policy and technical forum for countries to discuss and address forest issues on a regional basis.

The purpose of EFC is to advise on the formulation of forest policy and to review and coordinate its implementation at the regional level; to exchange information and, generally through special Subsidiary Bodies, to advise on suitable practices and action with regard to technical and economic problems, and to make appropriate recommendations in relation to the foregoing. It meets every two years and English, French and Spanish are the official languages of the Commission.

The EFC has a number of associated subsidiary bodies, including the Working Party on the Management of Mountain Watersheds, the Working Party on Mediterranean forestry issues (Silva Mediterranea) and shares with ECE the ECE/FAO Working Party on Forest Statistics, Economics and Management.

FAO encourages wide participation of government officials from forestry and other sectors as well as representatives of international, regional and subregional organizations that deal with forest-related issues in the region, including NGOs, and the private sector. Accordingly, EFC is open to all Members and Associate Members whose territories are situated wholly or in part in the European Region or who are responsible for the international relations of any non-self-governing territory in that Region. Membership comprises such eligible Member Nations as have notified the Director-General of their desire to be considered as Members.

EFC is one of the technical commissions serving to the FAO Regional Office for Europe and Central Asia (REU) and the EFC Secretary is based in Geneva. EFC work is regulated by Rules of Procedures, which were adopted by the FAO Conference in 1961 and amended at the Eighteenth Session of the Commission in 1977.

More information about the Commission's work may be obtained by contacting:

UNECE/FAO Forestry and Timber Section

Forests, Land and Housing Division

United Nations Economic Commission for Europe/

Food and Agriculture Organization of the United Nations

Palais des Nations

CH-1211 Geneva 10, Switzerland

info.ECE-FAOforests@un.org

www.unece.org/forests

Information Service
United Nations Economic Commission for Europe

Palais des Nations
CH - 1211 Geneva 10, Switzerland
Telephone: +41(0)22 917 12 34
Fax: +41(0)22 917 05 05
E-mail: unece_info@un.org
Website: http://www.unece.org